Sailors' ˹

Thanks mainly to the novels of C S Forester, Patrick O'Brian and Dudley Pope, there has been a upsurge of interest in the navy and sea life in the age of sail. This new series of contemporary memoirs and autobiographies fully supports the old notion that truth is stranger than fiction, since the best of the sailors' own tales are just as entertaining, informative and amusing, while they shed faithful light on the curious and outlandish world of the seaman. Avoiding the oft-reprinted or anthologised pieces, 'Sailors' Tales' offers only the rarest and most authentic accounts; but just as importantly they have been selected for their entertainment value, much enhanced in these newly designed editions.

THE NARRATIVE

OF

WILLIAM SPAVENS

A Chatham Pensioner

Written by himself

*A Unique Lower Deck View
of the Navy of the Seven Years War*

Introduction by N A M Rodger

CHATHAM PUBLISHING

LONDON

Publisher's Note
The typography of this edition has been updated
from the original eighteenth-century style, although in
the main the author's spelling has been retained to keep
the flavour of the original. Some modern spellings have
been introduced to increase clarity.

This edition published in Great Britain by
Chatham Publishing, 61 Frith Street, London W1V 5TA

Chatham Publishing is an imprint of Gerald Duckworth & Co Ltd

First published in 1796 by R. Sheardown, Louth,
for the benefit of the author

British Library Cataloguing in Publication Data
A catalogue record for this book is available
from the British Library

ISBN 1 86176 083 3

Introduction © N A M Rodger 1998

Type format of this edition © Chatham Publishing 1998

Original edition kindly provided by the
British Library: shelfmark 533D44

Typeset by Inde-Dutch Systems (India) Ltd

Printed and bound in Great Britain by
The Cromwell Press, Trowbridge, Wilts

Contents

Introduction

It is always hard for the historian to catch the voices and understand the feelings of the common people, and none are more elusive than the common seamen. Many of them illiterate, most of them unlettered, employed in an arduous profession which left little leisure for inessential reading and writing, they present them present themselves to the historian chiefly through the observations of officers, passengers and other outsiders; or in the artificial circumstances of lawsuits and courts martial at which they might give evidence; or, most commonly, as the drunken merrymakers whose antics on a run ashore filled up so many columns of eighteenth-century newspapers. What lower-deck memoirs we have come mostly from the end of that century, the time of the 'Great Wars' against France, and with few exceptions they were written long afterwards, often from very imperfect memory, and with a strongly didactic purpose. They are less impartial chronicles of time past than contributions to the religious, social or political debates of the 1830s and 1840s. Historians have for long used them with more eagerness than discretion. By contrast, very little attention has been given to this obscure but valuable *Narrative*. It was published in a small country town, presumably in a small edition; only a handful of copies are known to exist.

William Spavens, by then a cripple, wrote his book to raise money to support himself, evidently at the suggestion of friends and supporters, who must have heard his stories of his life at sea. It seems that he wrote his narrative proper, the memoir of his seafaring life, found it was too short to make up a book, and added sections describing the Navy and the merchant service, the geography of some of the towns and countries he had visited, and miscellaneous astronomical and scientific information, all interspersed with some further stories from his life. The result is not very well organised, but it is obviously the work of an intelligent and observant man with a reasonably good education. It is not clear how and when he acquired it, but he was clearly a man accustomed all his life to read and to think, master of a plain but expressive

English style. He was able to pass in respectable company without being suspected to be a common seaman, he mentions having books in his sea chest, and he discusses such questions as naval tactics with an understanding at least equal to that of the average naval officer of his day. He evidently had a particular interest in languages. His accurate remarks on spoken Manx and Norwegian, and on Chinese writing, suggest that he had taken pains to inform himself, and he had a working command of (phonetically-spelled) Dutch. His memory for names and dates, though not quite infallible, is so remarkably accurate as to suggest that he had somehow managed to save some sort of notes or diary, in spite of the several occasions on which he abandoned or lost most of his possessions. His spelling of proper names is somewhat casual, but there were admirals of his generation who could not do as well. Some parts of his description of the Royal Navy (for example the references to fire-ships, and to ketch-rigged bomb vessels) which were out of date when he published them in 1796, but accurately recall his time at sea forty years before, suggest that he was relying on memory, with or without some notes to assist it.

Above all, Spavens possessed the two talents which make a writer of memoirs especially valuable: he had the luck to find himself in interesting situations, and the imagination to realise what was interesting. To this we owe his striking account of the battle of Quiberon Bay, and the numerous vivid details of life at sea. He had first-hand experience of being pressed, and serving in a press-gang; he deserted from both a man-of-war and an East Indiaman. Best of all, he does not simply recount the facts, but tells us why he acted as he did, and what he felt about events, at the time and afterwards. He served under several colourful officers whose careers have been studied, including Captain Penhallow Cuming, 'an excellent seaman, but extremely rigid in his discipline', who was subsequently dismissed the Service for brutality. He was briefly under the future Lord Barham, and tells an anecdote discreditable to his seamanship.

All this is recounted with vigour and clarity, at times with real poetry. His description of the great victory of 'the gallant and swift-winged Hawke'; his passing evocation of English Harbour, 'where the water is so clear that I have seen fishes amongst the weeds as intelligible as though there had been no more than 3 feet depth of water'; his comment on slaves in the West Indies, 'Some of these people are of as bright a genius as those that rule over them'; all bespeak a man who could think and write for himself, a vivid witness of an age when very few wrote from his perspective, or his experience.

N A M Rodger
London 1998

The Author's Address to the Public

The circumscribed limits of my proposals have obliged me to omit several useful and entertaining particulars, together with many pleasing anecdotes; neither have I been able to give full scope to what is inserted: But should my endeavours meet with the approbation of a candid and generous public, so far as to render a second edition necessary, I hope to correct and enlarge it at a very small advancement in the price. I intended to have printed a list of my subscribers' names, (being about 520 in number, amongst whom are many very respectable Characters) but some of them, for reasons best known to themselves, having intimated a desire that their names should not be made use of; and it being very probable that some others of them may have the same desire; and as the work has unavoidably exceeded the limits of the price proposed, I flatter myself those who wished to have seen their names inserted will excuse me in the omission of them, sincerely thanking each of them for their support. And should any Gentleman of science observe any material inaccuracy or mistake in my little performance, I hope he will have candour enough to put a favourable construction upon it; and could I be favoured with his assistance in correcting it, nothing could be more grateful and obliging to

His humble Servant,

W. S.

A Dialogue between the Author and the Printer

Author   I hope, Mr Printer, as I am now favoured with a respectable list of subscribers, you will put my book to the press with all the expedition you can.

Printer   You need not doubt it. But do you intend to have neither Preface nor Dedication?

Author   I am so much a novice in the mystery of book-making, that I cannot conceive their utility.

Printer.   Give me leave to point out their use. I once had the curiosity to count over the sheets of a Preface, and found them nearly equal to half the Book: Now please to observe, that such long prefaces (though nobody reads them) may be very useful to an Author; for, if he cannot extend his subject to a sufficient bulk, he may swell his preface with any extraneous matter; besides, he there tells his readers his motives for publishing: (They may believe him if they please) He never intended his writings for the press; but some friends accidentally seeing his manuscript, desired him to publish it, and he, good-natured soul, could not refuse them.

Author.   Hold! No long Preface for me; and as to my motive for publishing, I frankly own it is to get a few shillings, which to a poor, old, mutilated Invalid, must be very acceptable, especially at a time when all the necessaries of life are excessively dear; but I shall think myself extremely happy if my poor abilities can produce any thing worthy of the perusal of my kind subscribers; if not, I beg leave to pour out the effusions of a grateful heart.

Printer.   But, respecting the Dedication – Is there no great Personage to whom you can inscribe your Book, and offer a profusion of adulation, and make the world believe that you and the Great Man are hand and glove?

Author.   Great Men seldom trouble their heads about the concerns of such a poor man as I am; for my station has been too humble and obscure to attract either public or private notice; besides flattery and deceit I utterly detest.

Printer.   But is there not ONE person in the whole World whose patronage you may solicit, and to whom, according to the usual manner of dedicating, you can make a public acknowledgement of favours received, without incurring the imputation of flattery and falsehood?

Author.   You now speak to my feelings: The many favours I have received from the worthy people of Louth and its vicinity, inspire me with the warmest sentiments of gratitude; it is a tribute due to their humanity, which I cannot withhold: I was languishing in pain, and pining in want, but they administered relief, and gave me every comfort my deplorable condition could receive; and now again they kindly step forward in supporting the publication of my Narrative. To them and the rest of my kind subscribers let my trifling Publication be humbly dedicated; I trust their Goodness will excuse its deficiencies.

The Seaman's Narrative

I was born at Stewton, a small village near Louth, in Lincolnshire, where my parents dying while I was very young, and leaving me unprovided for, Mr Gwillam, a respectable farmer of that place, took me into his family, where I lived about three years, and met with the kindest treatment. Some years after I lived with a farmer at Clee Thorps, where frequently having a view of Ships sailing by on the Humber, I thought sailors must be happy men to have such opportunities of visiting foreign countries, and beholding the wonderful works of the Creator in the remote regions of the earth; I considered not the perils and hardships they are sometimes exposed to; I thought of nothing but pleasant gales and prosperous voyages, and indulging a curiosity which seemed implanted in my nature. – Such were my thoughts of a seafaring life, though I did not intend to make trial of it immediately; but the term of my engagement with my master being expired, I hired myself to another, of whom I heard such an unfavourable character, that I determined not to serve him, but try my fortune on the watery element. I therefore went over to Hull, where I was highly delighted with a view of the ships in the harbour; and while I was gazing at them, a gentleman came and asked me if I would go to sea: I told him I had no objection, if I could meet with a master who would engage me. He took me to his house, and told his son to shew me his vessel, that I might see how I liked her. I went with him indeed; but one ship was the same to me as another: It was the vocation of a sailor that had engaged my attention, and it was a matter of indifference to me what vessel I sailed in. We speedily returned, and terms were proposed, which I readily accepted, though the gentleman advised me to go a voyage upon trial. I told him there was no necessity for it, as I had already made up my mind, and wished to have the indentures executed as soon as convenient, which was accordingly done; and on the 19th of May, 1754. I was bound apprentice to Mr Charles Wood, master and principal owner of the snow, *Elizabeth and Mary*, belonging to the port of Hull. Two or three days after, we set sail for Narva in Russia; I thought myself happy so far to have accomplished my wishes as to be now on a voyage; but I quickly found that the flattering prospect of my imaginary happiness was subject to be overcast with clouds; for the next day I was taken ill, but thought it was nothing more than a little sea-sickness: However my disorder proved to be the small-pox, which I had in so favourable a manner, that in fifteen days time, when we had reached our destined port, I was well enough to do such duty as was assigned me, and was generally employed in cooking; but the carpenter wanting to caulk the ship, I was ordered to heat the pitch-kettle, which was not allowed to be done on board, as we lay alongside the wharf, and the warehouses being built of wood, and stored with combustible commodities; I therefore went to the side of a hill at a little distance, which had a cavity at the top, filled with water; but the pitch taking fire, I ran to the top of the hill, and filling my hat with water, poured it on the flaming kettle, which made it rage with much greater fury, and brought one of the ship's crew to extinguish it; for had it been perceived by the Fitzhookers, who are a kind of custom-house officers, they would perhaps have had me severely punished.—Narva is a large town bordering on the gulf of Finland. The principal exports from this place are flax, timber, and corn. There is a remarkable waterfall at some distance above the town, where the river being upwards of one hundred yards wide, the water falls perpendicularly down a rock about twelve feet; the noise whereof may be heard at many miles distance. Above the water-fall is a grand Saw-mill, where timber being floated down the river above is stopped, and sawn into beams, planks, or deals, and then launched into the river below, and towed down to the sea to be taken on board the ships in the road.

We took in a cargo of flax, which it seems the Russian peasantry, for want of better accommodations, constantly sleep amongst so long as it remains in their possession; and the swarms of lice which appeared on our jackets when we stowed it into our vessel, gave me an unfavourable idea of the condition of those poor wretches.

This being my first voyage, and at so early a period of life, it cannot be expected I could gain much knowledge of the place, or become acquainted with the manners and customs of its inhabitants: I shall therefore reserve a more particular account of such matters for the second part of my pamphlet, where my readers will find them briefly treated of, either from my own observations, or the communications of those on whose veracity I thought I might safely depend; but in this place I shall content myself with relating such incidents as happened on shipboard, or such adventures on shore as engaged my young and inexperienced mind.

My next voyage was to Gottenburg in Sweden, where we took in a cargo of iron and deals. Here we found an excellent harbour, which lying without the sound, is well situated for foreign trade. In this country are many silver, copper, and iron mines. The exports are boards, gunpowder, leather, iron, copper, tallow, &c. The fishery here afforded such a plentiful supply of herrings, that we bought forty for a Stiver.

On our passage home, we had a hard gale, which continued eight days, and our vessel frequently shipping very heavy seas, every thing loose was washed off the deck, and we could have no fire all the time, and were therefore obliged to subsist on raw flesh, which made the master exclaim that a man had better be a fish than a sailor, excepting the little time he is on shore. If such were the sentiments of a man inured to the sea, what must my thoughts be on the occasion, who had never experienced such hardships before? Dreadful indeed are the dangers to which poor seamen are frequently exposed! I beg leave here to quote Mr Hervey's description of a tempest; for though I have often experienced the rough treatment of the roaring winds and raging billows, yet I cannot describe the distress they occasion in such forcible language as he has done. 'Navies,' says he, 'are rent from their anchors; and, with all their enormous load are whirled swift as the arrow, wild as the winds along the vast abyss. – Now they climb the rolling mountain; they plough the frightful ridge, and seem to skim the skies. Anon they plunge into the opening gulph; they lose the sight of day, and are lost themselves to every eye. How vain is the pilot's art! how impotent the mariner's strength! They reel to and fro, and stagger in the jarring hold; or cling to the cordage, while bursting seas foam over the deck. *Despair* is in every face, and *death* sits threatening on every surge.' He then admonishes them to implore the protection of the Almighty, whose power alone can save them – It is their only resource – their last effort to secure their eternal salvation; but it is like a death-bed repentance, and their sincerity can only be judged of by the searcher of hearts.

I have somewhere seen it observed, that when sailors are in such distress that they have scarcely any hopes of saving their lives, they will curse the elements, go to prayer, and make the most solemn vows of amendment, which are generally forgotten as soon as the tempest is over; but, to the honour of my brother tars, I can truly assert, that I have met with many humane and worthy characters in the service, who I have reason to suppose were neither wanting in their duty to their God nor their fellow creatures.

My next voyage was to Havre de Grace with a cargo of lead. Whilst we were there, a report was spread, that there was likely to be a rupture betwixt England and France; on which a Frenchman observed, that his countrymen were very kind to the English to buy their lead, and give them it back for nothing; to which, answer was made, that the English are so generous a people, it need not be doubted but they will return the favour with interest.

On our return, we did not come through the Downs, and wished to shun Yarmouth Road to avoid the press; but the wind veering and blowing a strong gale, we were forced in, and soon after boarded by a boat belonging to the *Augusta*'s tender, and two of our crew were impressed; and when we reached Hull, I shared the same fate, and was hauled on board the *John and Joyce*, tender to the *Colloden*.

During my confinement, a scheme was formed by the impressed men, to take the ship from the crew, and run her on shore to regain their liberty; but the plot being discovered, Lieutenant Kirby sent notice of it to Captain Smelt (the regulating Captain on shore) to send him a reinforcement, which he no sooner received than he doubled the guards, giving them positive orders to fire amongst us if we attempted to mutiny. After this we were all confined below every night, and in the day-time only two of us were suffered to come upon deck at once. Our confinement in this floating prison lasted thirty-two days; after which we were happily released and put on board His Majesty's ship the *Buckingham* of 70 guns, commanded by the Honourable Temple West, Rear Admiral of the Red. This being the first day, we employed it in slinging our hammocks; and the next morning all hands being called on deck, one of the boatswain's mates told me I must now become a sky-lark and mount up aloft; I therefore ascended the foretop with much pleasure, flattering myself I should now make great improvement as a sailor. When we had completed our stores and rigging, and got our guns on board, we sailed round to Spithead to join Sir Edward Hawke, Vice Admiral of the White. Here we lay till the beginning of July, and being increased to the number of thirty-five sail, His Royal Highness the Duke of Cumberland came to review the fleet; and on that occasion, Lord Anson, Admiral of the Blue, came down and hoisted his flag on board the *Prince* of 90 guns; and then His Royal Highness put off in the commissioner's barge with twelve oars, and was followed by the three Admirals' barges; next went the Captains in their barges all ranged in due order according to their seniority; after them the Lieutenants in the pinnaces; and the Masters, Mates, Midshipmen, &c, in yawls and cutters. The yards and stays both fore and aft were manned through the whole fleet, with a man also at each topgallant-mast head. The long train of gallant ships with the men thus displayed, was, to me, a new and pleasing sight; but standing so long in an erect position on the yards, I must confess was rather painful.

As soon as the Duke came on board the *Prince*, the blue flag was struck, and the royal standard hoisted, and the *Prince* firing a gun, the whole fleet gave a royal salute, each ship firing twenty-one guns. This we termed a Spithead fight, and thought it would have been without bloodshed, but in that we were mistaken; for unfortunately the *Medway*'s main top-gallant lift gave way, and let twelve men fall, some on the deck and the rest into the water, by which accident some lost their lives, and others were very much hurt. The beach was crowded with spectators, who dispersed as soon as his Royal Highness returned on shore.

Our naval parade being now ended, we got ready for sea, and with sixteen sail of the line, and the *Ambuscade* and *Gibraltar* frigates went out to cruise in the bay of Biscay, in quest of a fleet commanded by Admiral Macnamara with a homeward-bound fleet of merchantmen under convoy; but, though they escaped us, we had great success in picking up a number of French vessels returning home from foreign ports; for as they had not received intelligence of the rupture between the two kingdoms, they did not attempt to avoid us, and so became an easy prey.

Finding a fleet of observation no longer necessary in the bay, we returned to England, and on the 30th of September put into Plymouth with part of the fleet (Sir Edward Hawke proceeding with the rest to Portsmouth) and after we had docked our ship and completed our stores, we fell down from Hamoaze into the Sound; but having above our complement of men, I and some others were sent on board the *Blandford* of 24 guns, which had been taken by Commodore Guay, and carried into Nantes, but was sent back by the French with a view to have the *Lys* of 50 guns and the *Alcide* of 64 restored by our ministry, they having been captured by our fleet under the command of Admirals Boscawen, Holborn, and Mostin, off Cape Breton in America. Sailing from Plymouth, we arrived at Spithead on the 5th of November, where we lay till the 30th of January following, and then set sail for the West Indies; and bringing to off the Eddistone, were joined by Rear Admiral Townsend in the *Dreadnought* of 60 guns. In our passage we touched at Madeira, the chief of the Canary islands, where we stayed some time to take in wine, water, &c.—This island appears like a stupendous hill, extending from east to west; the clouds seem beneath its summit. The south declivity of this hill is cultivated, and delightfully interspersed with vineyards and most kinds of tropical and european fruits; the hedges are adorned with myrtles, roses, jessamine, and honey-suckles, in continual bloom; many kinds of beautiful flowers spring up spontaneously, and the country seats of the merchants promiscuously scattered about, form a delightful prospect. The Madeira wines are so well known as to need no description.

Leaving Madeira, we sailed in company with the *Dreadnought*, till we had passed the Tropic, when we parted from her, she steering for Jamaica and we for Barbados, where arriving on the 1st of April, we found the *Winchester*, the Captain whereof informed us that the *Warwick* was taken by a squadron of French men of war off Dominica. This island is said to be about twenty-five miles long and fifteen broad. It produces sugar, rum, molasses, ginger, cotton, &c. Its principal fruits are pineapples, oranges, lemons, citrons, limes, figs, tamarinds, cocoa-nuts, pomegranates, &c. It abounds also with hogs, cows, oxen, and horses, and some sheep are kept, but the mutton is inferior to that we have in England. Poultry and wild fowl are also plentiful. The bays afford excellent fish, such as the parrot-fish, cavelloes, snappers, flying-fish, and many others. A short description of the flying-fish may perhaps be agreeable to such of my readers as are not conversant in natural history: It is about the length of a herring, but thicker and rounder; and its fins being large and flexible, when they are expanded they serve in some measure the purpose of wings, so long as they remain wet; but as soon as they become dry, they grow stiff, and the fish falls again into the water, except its fins are moistened by dashing against the spray, and then it will take another flight. I have sometimes seen them fly on board of a ship when they have been pursued by the dolphins, which prey upon them in the water; and if they fly out of that element, they are frequently caught by the boobies which hover above the water to devour them; but notwithstanding that many of them are thus constantly destroyed, they are still found here in great plenty, and are excellent food.

After we had been some time here, we sailed for Antigua, and to windward of Guadaloupe fell in with three sail of line of battle-ships detached from the squadron which had a little before taken the *Warwick*, and chasing us, we ran into English harbour for safety; but our fears were quickly over, as Admiral Frankland arrived with a squadron from Europe, which gave us the superiority in the Leeward Islands.

War being declared against France on the 12th of May, 1756, we went on a cruise about sixty leagues east of Barbuda, and fell in with and took the *Pacific* of six hundred tons burden, mounting 16 guns, laden with flour, wine, shoes, and pickled geese, bound to St Domingo, and belonged to Bourdeaux.

About forty leagues to windward of Barbados, we came up with two outward-bound English ships, and as the coasts swarmed with French privateers, our Captain engaged to escort them safe in with the land. The next day we discovered two schooners and a sloop privateer in chase of us. Having ordered the merchant ships ahead of us, we hoisted Dutch colours, going under an easy sail, till two of the French vessels being within point blank shot of us, gave us a smart salute, which we seemed to take little notice of till the other ship came up, and then hauling down the Dutch colours, and hoisting the English, we returned their compliment in such a manner that they seemed perfectly satisfied; and putting out their oars, and hauling close to the wind, they hastily bade us adieu. The construction of these ships was so well adapted for flight, that we found it in vain to attempt to chase them. We then bore away with the ships we had in charge into Carlisle bay, where we left them, and again beat to windward, and one day relieved a ship which had been chased sixty leagues.

After having made several unsuccessful trips, we were ordered to heave down in the English harbour to have our ship cleaned, for her bottom was become so foul, that we could come up with nothing we gave chase to.

During our being in harbour, there was a hurricane which bore down almost everything before it, and the sea rose so high that it broke over the horse-shoe battery. After the tempest abated, the *Edinburgh* and *Anson* came into harbour; the former under jury-masts, having carried all by the board, and the latter with her fore-mast sprung, having had all her sails blown from the yards. Whilst we were careening our ship, Captain Richard Watkins, who had married Colonel Lasley's daughter, having a house at St John's, spent so much of his time there, that Admiral Frankland not approving of his conduct, sent a remonstrance, and ordered him immediately to return; to which the captain sending a contumacious answer, he was, by order of the Admiral, arrested and made a prisoner, and afterwards tried by a Court Martial for contempt, disobedience, and neglect of duty, and was suspended and ordered home; and the Admiral made Mr Penhallow Cummings (then master and commander of the *Saltash* sloop) Post Captain, and appointed him to the command of our ship; and also made Mr Charles Middleton (now Admiral Middleton) master and commander, and gave him the command of the *Speaker* Brig; but neither the *Saltash* nor *Speaker* being there, Mr Middleton commanded our ship till we met with the *Saltash*.

Soon after this, we captured a schooner privateer called *Le Victorie* of 14 guns and 80 men, and the next morning retook an English snow, and carried them into Montserat; but not finding an approved agent there, we again put to sea with them, and went to St Christopher's; and on our return to windward, we took a sloop privateer of 10 guns and 50 men, which we carried to St John's; where finding the *Saltash*, Mr Middleton resigned the command of our ship to Captain Cummings; and, according to his appointment, took the command of the *Speaker*, with which vessel we sailed in company on a cruise to windward of Barbados, and gave chase to a schooner privateer, which led us many leagues to the leeward; and on coming up with her, Mr Middleton endeavoured to gain the commission, by being the first on board of her, which is not only a point of honour, but also a matter of interest: He therefore hoisted out his boat, with all sails set, going at the rate of ten knots, by which he filled the boat with water, and with difficulty saved the lives of the two men that were in her, although he immediately threw all his sails to the masts. This gave us an advantage, which we made the best use of, and had the honour of gaining the prize which the others had risked their lives for. Many bets were made as we passed Carlisle bay respecting which of the two, the ship or the brig, would first come up with the chase.

Our cruise being out, we returned to English harbour; and a transport with soldiers on board, (destined to reinforce Lord Louden's corps in North America) having sprung a leak at sea, and running for Antigua, put in there; and the soldiers were placed in the garrison at Monk's Hill till a suitable vessel could be procured for them to proceed in; but none being found, the Admiral ordered us to take them on board and carry them to New York, where we arrived on the 9th of April, 1757. In our passage thither, a soldier's wife was delivered of a boy who was named Blandford, after our ship.—New York is an exceeding fine city, advantageously seated on a point between the north and west rivers, which join at the south east end of the town, and fall into the sea at sandy hook. It is the mart of commerce for the state of New York, and might vie with several of the commercial cities in Europe to which it has an extensive trade. The country abounds with grain and various kinds of fruit and vegetables. The river affords plenty of oysters, but being fresh water, they are too lucious to eat raw, but are excellent when stewed. After some time spent here, we returned to Carlisle bay, where our Captain devised means to disguise the ship, in order to deceive the privateers, as many of them had got to know her; and they being mostly Bermudian-built vessels, properly constructed for running, and always kept clean, and their bottoms payed with a composition of chalk and tallow, they had much the advantage of us in swiftness of sailing; we therefore had a false stern made to ship and unship at pleasure, and a bonnet made to the jib which we could take off, and the sail being set without it, had the appearance of a Dutchman's small spitfire jib, and hoisting Dutch colours, the privateers were sometimes deceived, and ventured nearer us than they otherwise would have done.

While we continued here, a sloop privateer came and looked into the bay, standing so close in, that they fired at her from Needham's Fort, on which our Captain came on board and determined to chase her. It was then two o'clock in the afternoon, and about one in the morning we came up with and took her; but she had led us so far to the leeward, that it took us a fortnight beating to windward before we got to Barbados. She proved the *Minerva* of Fort Royal, Martinico. I and some others went on board this prize which we found in a wretched condition, for she was so leaky we could scarcely keep her afloat, and they had slacked all the lanyards of the shrouds, knocked out the wedges of the masts, and sawn the gunwales through into the ports to increase her speed in their flight, so that she appeared as if she would go to pieces under our feet. The French Captain, who had but one hand, was a very polite and ingenuous man. He told us he had taken our ship for an African trader, and intended to have cut her out in the night.

I cannot say that our accommodations on board the prize were very comfortable, for we had no bedding, and nowhere to sleep but on the water-casks in the hold, where we were so infested with the mosquittos and sand-flies that we could get little rest; nor was our situation upon deck more eligible, for it blew so hard that we were continually wet.

After coming to Barbados, we put our prisoners on shore, and chose an agent, who sent a prize-master on board to take charge of the *Minerva*; and having got a supply of water, we set off again in search of new adventures.

About fifty leagues north east of Antigua, we saw and gave chase to another sloop privateer which we followed from ten o'clock in the morning till three o'clock next day, when she running close in with the island of Barbuda, led into shoal water, where we could not follow her, and so was forced to give up the chase after we had fired upwards of a hundred 9lb shot from two guns pointed out of the head doors as chase-guns. She once was so near under our bow, that we fired at her with muskets from the fore-castle and off the fore-yard, by which we shot away the earing of her square fail and her ringtail tack; but they quickly repaired the damage, and the wind dying away, she was soon out of our reach.

Our former Captain having been suspended, as I mentioned before, Captain Cummings succeeded him in the command of the

Blandford. He was an excellent seaman, but extremely rigid in his discipline, and would frequently withhold the mens' allowance of grog on the most trifling occasions. I have known him call all hands to sway up the main top gallant yard, which ten men would have effected with ease; and if we were not all upon deck in five minutes, he would place a petty officer at every hatchway to stop those who remained below, and would order each man a dozen lashes at the gangway for his tardiness. He would also on the least provocation being given him by any of the quartermasters, boatswain's mates, midshipmen, or other Petty Officers, break them and turn them before the mast, disrate them of their wages, and sometimes flog them.

After making a few trips, in which nothing remarkable happened, we were again ordered into English harbour, where Commodore Moore arriving to take the command (Admiral Frankland being recalled) and bringing with him a fleet of merchant ships bound to Jamaica, ordered us immediately to take in all our stores and guns, and escort the fleet to Port Royal, and there put ourselves under the command of Rear Admiral Coats, who soon after our arrival, ordered us to convoy two brigantines laden with slaves to Carthagena, and the value of their cargoes being to be paid for in bullion, or uncoined gold, we proceeded to Porto-Bello for it.—This is but a mean place, yet fortified with much care and expence, and is of great advantage to the Spaniards; for being situate on the north east side of the isthmus of Darien, whence it is but ninety miles across to Panama, it is much easier and safer for them to bring their bullion thither on mules, and transport it in guarda costas to La Vera-Cruz, to be put on board their register ships for Cadiz, that to have it brought through the stormy seas round Cape Horn, or sent across the Pacific Ocean, and then home.

In our passage to Porto-Bello, we were alarmed with the appearance of a water-spout at a little distance on our weather-bow; it seemed to approach us very fast, and we were preparing our guns to fire at it, but it began to weaken, and quickly dispersed, letting fall such a body of water, that had our ship been under it, she must have sunk. They are frequent on this coast, and their first appearance is a dark cloud, which extends itself into the form of an inverted cone or sugar-loaf, the small end pointing to the sea, and stretching out like a huge funnel, which no sooner comes in contact with the water, but it appears greatly agitated, and a large body of it is drawn up into the clouds, which becoming overcharged, it generally falls again in the rapid manner I have described. This phænomenon I suppose is caused by the whirling round of the clouds, acted upon by contrary winds meeting in a point, nearly in the same manner as dust, straw, &c. are raised by a whirlwind at land.—This country abounds with various kinds of tropical fruits, which spring up spontaneously, and frequently drop from the trees, and remain to rot on the ground. Large birds of the Pelican kind are frequently seen here flying about the harbour, and prey upon the fish, which they will dart down upon and catch several feet under water. The beak of one of these birds cut off at the eyes, might be so extended as to draw over a man's head like a night-cap. I saw one of the largest alligators here that ever I met with.

After we had received on board the wedges and bars of gold brought us from Panama, we sailed for Carthagena, and in a few days arrived in Bucha Chica road, and anchored close under the guns of the castle, but were not suffered to go into the harbour; however the Spanish governor behaved to us with great politeness; made our Captain several handsome presents, and sent two small bullocks and fourteen large tortoises for the use of our ships company; but we had no other means allowed us to procure water, than by sinking a cask in the sand for a well, near the castle, which was the very spot where the bones of the forces which co-operated with Admiral Vernon's fleet in 1740 were deposited.

Our Captain having stopped as much of our allowance of rum as he sold at Porto-Bello for 20l. 8s. bought a few cigars here, and served them amongst us, saying, that smoking would prevent those disorders the humidity of the climate might occasion; he also gave us two days provision of fresh beef; but after our return to Jamaica, he sold all the salt beef and pork that was due to us; and the money which arose from the sale thereof, as well as the beasts and tortoises given us by the Spanish governor, he appropriated to his own use.

Coming again to Port Royal, Admiral Coats ordered our Captain to take in charge a homeward-bound packet and some vessels bound to America. In our passage, we fell in with and took three sail of large Dutch ships, and a brig of three hundred tons burden, laden with sugars, rum, coffee, cocoa, cochineal, cotton, indigo, &c. which were consigned to Bourdeaux, but they sailed so. heavily they could not keep up with the fleet; and as going at such a slow rate would retard the voyage of those vessels we had taken under convoy, the Captain of the packet, and the masters of the homeward-bound ships, agreed to run their passage without us, that we might wait to conduct our prizes securely into port. But about fifteen leagues eastward of Port Marant, we discovered a conspiracy which had been projected on board one of the Dutch ships; for the governor of Port au Prince's lady being a passenger, she advised them to keep as far behind our ship as they could, without causing suspicion; and when it was dark, to seize our Lieutenant and his men, and throw them overboard; and the Dutch mate to take the command, and make all the sail he could north-ward; conjecturing that we would not hazard losing the three other ships to pursue theirs, which we might suppose to be at a consider-able distance, and not easily found, as we could not know for a certainty what course they would take. But the lady making use of the French language in her conversation with the Dutch mate, &c. our second Lieutenant understanding French, discovered their plot; and, ordering the man at the wheel to luff nearer to the ship, one of the Dutchmen gave the man at the helm a blow, and strove to take the wheel out of his hand, when Mr Mowat (for that was the name of the Lieutenant) hailed us, informed us of their design, and desired immediate assistance, as our men on board the Dutch vessel were too few to cope with the prisoners if they were resolved to mutiny. On which we sent out a boat with a sufficient force to quell them; and the Mate, Boatswain, and principal ringleaders were brought on board our ship, put in irons, and kept separate from the other prisoners. We then set sail, and carried them safe into Port Royal; and choosing Samuel Bean, Esq. and Mr Papley of Kingston, as our agents, we worked them up to that place; and leaving a Midshipman on board of each ship, and appointing Mr Sprat (whom the Captain had caused to be tried by a Court Martial held on board the *Marlborough* between our coming from Carthagena and going out with the packet, &c.) to superintend the whole, we prepared for another cruise. Before we left this place, the *Augusta* came triumphantly in with nine sail of prizes, which she alone had captured all together, eight of them being stout ships, and the other a brig.

We were next ordered to cruize off Cape Francois, where we were daily either chasing or were chased by Rhode island and other American privateers; we therefore spoke with many of them, and agreed upon signals, by which we might be able to distinguish our friends from our foes: In the day time an ensign was to be placed on the fore-top mast head, and in the night six false fires were to be displayed on the quarter deck. This we found prevented many inconveniences, and saved us much unnecessary trouble. We some-times stretched in close under the forts to get a view of the harbour; and after cruising here about a month, took a Dutch sloop from Curiso, but examining her papers, let her go again. After that, we took a Dutch schooner, called the *Prince William*, which we retained; and three days after, we took another Dutch schooner, called the *Industry*, which we manned and kept with us till we cap-tured two more schooners, one a Dane, and the other a Spaniard, when we bore away with our four little prizes to Jamaica, where we found that the court of admiralty at Kingston had condemned two of the Dutch ships that we had before carried into Port Royal, but the other being cleared, proceeded on her voyage. We now went to Kingston to land the cargoes of our prizes, when the Captain find-ing something amiss in the conduct of the Master, he again confined him as a prisoner, notwithstanding he had been hon-ourably acquitted of his former charge. Having finished our business at this place, we fell down to Greenwich to take in some stores; and here the Captain caused the Boatswain (Mr Richard Lee) to absent himself from the service, ordering the boat to put him ashore. When we returned to Port Royal, we found the admi-ralty court had released the Dane and Spaniard, but adjudged the two Dutch vessels to be legal prizes. The Captain now caused the *Industry*, which was New England built, and a prime sailor, to be fitted up for a tender to the ship, for the purpose of running close in shore after small vessels, which by reason of their small draught of water, could easily get out of the ship's way. Mr William Husband had the command of this tender, which mounted 16 swivel guns, and had 20 men; and I was appointed gunner's mate. But the trade being now ready to sail for Europe, the Admiral appointed the *Lynn* of 44 guns, and the *Sphinx* of 24 guns, as a convoy; yet the merchants petitioning for a stronger force to escort so valuable a fleet, we were ordered to join them; and sailing from Port Royal on the 20th of June, 1758, we anchored at Bluefields the day following, where we watered, and were joined by the trade from Peak Bay, Savannah, La Mar, &c. Leaving Bluefields with about three hundred sail in company, great and small (some of which were only going to America) a few nights after our departure, the thunder and lightening being so violent, we were in imminent danger of running foul of each other; for the flashes were so glaring as to make our eyes dim, and the intervals so exceeding dark, that to prevent accidents, some vessels kept tinkling bells, others beating drums; and those which had neither, made a noise on the deck with handspikes. Providentially no disaster happened to any of the fleet.

The Captain having given directions and positive orders to Mr Husband [master's mate,] respecting the order of sailing, to keep the *Industry* a point and a half on his weather-bow, and at a mile and a half distance; and to Mr James Blake, the other master's mate, commanding the other schooner, to keep one point and a half under his lee-bow, and at the same distance as the other, appointing signals to each; and our vessel going as if she had been in ballast, he would make our signal every evening to run round the fleet, and gather in the stragglers, by making the headmost shorten sail, and the sternmost make more sail; so that we were almost constantly employed. One day while we were at dinner, our signal (a white pendant at the mizzen peak) had been flying some time unperceived, when the whizzing of a nine-pound shot, fired from the ship disturbed our repast, and before we could bear down it was followed by another; then putting our helm a weather, we wore, and came under his stern. He then taking the speaking trumpet, hailed, saying, 'Mr Husband! why don't you observe my signals?' and ordered him to make all the sail he could, and steer W. S. W. till sunset, in order to make some small islands called the Granadillas, lying S. W. of Cuba, and to set the bearing of the fleet before we lost sight of it, that we might know how to steer for it in the morning; so we spread all our canvas, and shaped our course according to his command; and by four o'clock lost sight of the fleet which then bore N. E. by N. distant about six leagues; and continuing our course as had been directed, till the sun was below the horizon, we hauled up N. W. that we might fall in ahead of the convoy. In the morning, a man going up the shrouds, cried out, 'the fleet,' but soon discovered his mistake, for the objects he beheld

were not a fleet of ships, but trees on the Cuba shore. We therefore
concluded we were far ahead; and seeing a sail under our lee, we
bore away to speak to her, and found her to be the Dutch fluyt
which we had before carried into Port Royal. On hailing her, the
Mate asked Captain Thompson if he was acquainted with the gulf,
and on being answered no, he said if he could keep up with us he
would see him safe through. The Dutchman thankfully accepted
his offer; but Mr Husband designed, if he could meet with a privateer in the bay of Mexico, to take possession of the *Livedee* and carry
her to Providence, where he thought Governor Tinker would condemn her at all events. However our water having been put into
rum casks, and kept whilst it stunk very much, and being also in
want of other necessaries, we one night deserted the vessel, telling
Mr Husband in the morning that we believed she had run ashore,
at which he seemed much disturbed, but had recourse to his usual
method of dispelling uneasiness – by hard drinking, which he followed up so closely, that it almost prevented him from taking the
necessary observations. Complaining of our water, &c. he proposed
carrying us to Mexico, or else to Havannah, but we objected to it,
supposing he had a design to sell the schooner, and turn us adrift
among the Spaniards. At the time we left Bluefields, he had fourteen gallons of rum of his own, besides his share of the ship's stock,
which being all expended, we refused to supply him with what
belonged to ourselves, telling him he had got his due, and must
expect no more. He replied he could not subsist without liquor, but
if we would consent to go to Providence, he would procure us a
supply; to this we consented, and let him partake of our allowance;
but falling into the current, it carried us through the gulf as far as
Beheima bank before we discovered that we were in it; so that
being now past Providence, we intended to have steered for
Charles Town, but fell in with Port Royal, which is about fifteen
leagues to the southward of it; and seeing a sail, we gave chase to it;
but Mr Husband thinking we did not set the sails with alacrity,
began to swear, saying, that if we did not obey his commands, he
would throw his books and instruments overboard, and we should
all go to hell together. Having come up with the Snow we were in
chase of, and which proved to be an English vessel, she accompanied us into the Rebellion road, and after that we proceeded to
Charles Town, and saluted Captain Hale of the *Winchelsea* of 13

guns, and I and another were ordered by our officer to put him on shore, which we did, and got some rum and fresh beef; but at night he returned in the pilot-boat, and coming along side of us, as I had the first watch, he ordered me to get up the runner and tackle, and call assistance to hoist up two hogsheads of sugar which had been taken out of the *Prince William* prize, and strike them over the side into the pilot-boat; but I told him the tackle was too much out of repair to do it: He then said we might put ten bags of coffee into her; but (suspecting he had a design to embezzle them) I said neither I nor he could justify such a proceeding. As I refused to obey his orders, he and the pilot went into the cabin, where they sat drinking till break of day, and then went on shore again, and we saw him no more till about a fortnight after, when seeing the *Blandford* coming over the bar, he came on board; and when the ship came to anchor, Captain Cummings observed Mr Husband walking about on the deck of the schooner, who not seeming to pay him a proper attention, he hailed him with a speaking trumpet, saying, 'Mr Husband, you seem as great a man as myself;' after which Mr Husband ordered us to put him on board the *Blandford*: And the Captain determining to take the schooners no farther, an agent was appointed, and they were disposed of. The *Blandford* only brought in four vessels under convoy, all the rest having been dispersed in a gale of wind.

Whilst the ship was in the Gulf of Mexico, our Captain put the first Lieutenant under confinement for sleeping on his watch, and Captain Hale sent us Mr George Gaborian, his second Lieutenant, to supply his place. We now sailed from this place in company with the *Winchelsea*, with thirty-five sail under convoy; but on the 6th of September we had a hard gale from W. S. W. which brought the whole fleet under their courses, and still increasing, and night coming on, the *Winchelsea* made a signal for bringing to, and each vessel got under such sail as she could lie to in the easiest manner. Our ship brought to under a balanced mizzen, and she being old and leaky, we were obliged to pump for our lives; and the water seemed to gain upon us, although we used both our chain and hand pumps, and baled the water out with buckets besides. About two o'clock in the morning, the tempest was so violent that we every moment expected to be buried in the deep; for the ship lay almost on her beam ends, and the water reached five strakes upon the main deck, and the sheet anchor being on the lee-bow, she lay motionless several minutes, as if she was going down; but at length shaking her head, she righted; and towards morning we got the pumps to suck. When it was light, a Snow in company foundered, but the crew were saved, excepting one man, who seemed more anxious to save his money than his life; for though he knew the vessel was going down, and saw the men crowding into the boat as fast as they possibly could, yet he ran to his chest to secure his treasure, and, poor wretch, his life was the forfeit of his temerity. Our ship lying just in the trough of the sea, the raging billows, like high mountains, seemed as if they would roll over our mastheads, and we could not discern the other ships at the distance of four cable lengths from us. Weathering our helm we put her before the wind, and scudded at first under our bare poles, till fourteen sail of the merchantmen saw and followed us, (the remainder still lying to with the *Winchelsea*, which had lost all her masts.) We then loosed the goose-wings of our foresail, and scudded under them to prevent the sea pooping us; and when the tempest rather abated, we set our close-reefed fore-top sail; and though our danger was over, but a few days after, we were threatened with another quite as alarming, though of a different nature: The Steward's books taking fire in his room just over the magazine, the ship must have been blown up, had not the purser been awake in his cabin in the gun-room; but he perceiving it, the fatal consequence that might have happened was prevented.

It continued to blow for some time, and when we arrived off Scilly, we had only four sail in company. The wind blowing down the channel, we put into St Mary's Sound; and while we were there, a ship came in from Malaga, which had been out so long, that her bottom was quite green, and her sails and rigging bleached white; the crew were so emaciated with continual fatigue, and their strength so much exhausted, that they could scarcely hold themselves on the yard; and one of them was so weak that he fell from the main yard as the ship came into the Sound. We sent out our long boat, with hands, to their assistance.

When the wind came westerly, we sailed again, and on the first of November anchored in Cawsand Bay, and the next day moved into Plymouth Sound, and in consequence of orders we received, went into Hamoaze, where the ship was surveyed, and found unfit for further service, and was therefore stripped and laid at moorings in Millbrook Cove. While we were here, a court martial was held on board the *Duke* for the trial of Mr Sprat, our Master, and Mr Grible, our Lieutenant; the result of which was the acquittal of the Master, and the breaking of the Lieutenant, but not so but that he might be restored again. No sooner had Captain T Hanway pronounced the sentence, but he produced an order from the admiralty court to try Captain Cummings on a charge of cruel and unwarrantable treatment of the officers and men under his command, and embezzling their allowance, &c. and particularly in sending the Boatswain out of the ship at Greenwich in Jamaica, and forcing him to leave the service; when the charges were proved, the Captain was broke of his command under the 32nd article of war, and rendered incapable of ever serving again in the capacity of an officer in His Majesty's service, his heirs and successors.

The *Blandford* now being laid in Rotten Row, part of our officers and men were sent on board the *Orford* of 70 guns, the rest remaining in our own ship till the *Vengeance* frigate of 28 guns (prize to the *Huzza*) was put into commission, and the command of her given to Captain Joseph Hunt, and then we were sent on board of her; and in January, 1759, being ordered to Ireland, we sailed for Dublin Bay, where we lay till April to procure men for the service, and were attended by two cutters and a wherry, in the latter of which we put about 20 men and an officer, and sometimes went to sea as far as the high land of Wicklow to reconnoitre the coast, and when we perceived a ship coming in, we concealed ourselves, and let only the wherry men be seen, who were pilots for the bar and polebeg; and one day as the *Dublin* Letter of Marque from New York was coming in, we sheered under her lee, asking if they wanted a pilot? the Captain said they did, and told us to come alongside; but the men having some suspicion of our design, bid us keep off, or they would fire upon us. Now making the signal to the ship, she loosed her top-sails and sheeted them home; we then fired several guns in order to bring her to, and sent the boat with an officer and a proper number of hands to go on board of her; the officer they admitted, but the men they refused. Having therefore small hopes of succeeding, we prosecuted our design no farther at this time, but when night came on, she stretched over towards the hill of Heath, but in the first watch came and brought up a-beam of us within a quarter of a mile distance, whereupon the Lieutenant ordered the cutter to row guard round her all night, and sent the yawl to the Captain at Dublin, who brought down the two cutters, and re-inforcing them from the ship, boarded the Letter of Marque, one on each quarter, while we with our yawl and cutter boarded her on each bow at the same instant; but finding the men had taken close quarters, we scuttled their decks with axes, and fired down amongst them, while they kept firing up at us where they saw the light appear. After having shot one of our men through the head, and another through both his thighs, they submitted, and we got 16 brave fellows. There was a woman and a child in a side cabin in the state room, neither of which had received any injury, although the ceiling above them was full of shot-holes. Such are the methods frequently made use of to obtain seamen for the service in this land of liberty. It seems shocking to the feelings of humanity, for a sailor, after he has been a long voyage, endured innumerable hardships, and is just returning to his native land with the pleasing hope of shortly beholding a beloved wife and children, some kind relations, or respected friends, to be forced away to fight, perhaps to fall, and no more enjoy those dear connexions – it is a hardship which nothing but absolute necessity can reconcile to our boasted freedom.

After touching at Cork, we arrived at Plymouth in May, and having delivered most of the new men to the guard-ship to be at the disposal of Vice Admiral Harrison, went into dock; and on our coming out again, the Admiral ordered Captain Hunt to quit the *Vengeance*, and take command of the *Unicorn*, and gave Captain Gemaliel Nightingale of the *Badger* sloop the command of our ship; and then we sailed again for Liverpool on the same service, where we joined two ships and two cutters tenders on the same employ. One of the cutters being cruising about Formby Sands, as the *Golden Lion* was coming in from the Greenland seas, made the signal of their not being able to board her, whereupon we loosed our top-sails, and fixed a slip bouy on the cable, and on her nearer approach, sheeting home the top-sails, prepared to slip; but, on perceiving the tender's boat alongside, as well as our own cutter, the first Lieutenant ordering the barge to be manned; and stepping into her himself, accompanied by the Master at Arms, we put off, and went alongside the *Lion*, where finding all quiet, the Lieutenant bade us stay in the boat till we were called; and having obtained the ship's book of Captain Thompson, mustered the crew, and they answered severally to their names; but a Topsom ship having been lost in the ice, and some of the men taken on board the *Lion* they lay concealed, which being unknown to the Master and Lieutenant, and the wind and tide favouring their design, they had not the least doubt of success; but when she had drifted nearly a-breast of the *Vengeance*, a man stepping aft, and righting the helm, said, fill the main top-sail, which alarming the Lieutenant, he ran to the gangway, saying, step in, my lads, and let go the anchor, which we immediately attempted to do; but as I ascended the side, I heard a man call to the people concealed below, to hand up; on which they were presently furnished with lances and flinching-knives, which beginning to make use of in their defence, we were obliged to jump into the boat again as fast as we could, and put off, left they should let some of their boats (which hung in the tackle) run upon us and sink us. They having taken our officers prisoners on the quarter deck, immediately made sail; and our ship slipping her cable, pursued them, firing several point blank shots till some of them striking the town, we desisted, and came to in the Slyne, the *Lion* having gained the dock, where being moored, and her sails furled, the prisoners were released, and taking them into our boat, put them on board the ship.

Pressing on shore at Liverpool had been deemed impracticable, and some gentlemen one day told our Captain they were certain he durst not attempt to do it; but soon after he came to the dock head, and stepping into the barge, ordered us to put off, and go on board; and when it was dark, sent us and the cutter's crew, with some officers and a suitable reinforcement of men, to try if it were possible to succeed or not. We accordingly began our business, and soon picked up 16 men, but only one of them being a seaman, him we detained, and the rest we set at liberty. The next day, July 25th, being their fair day, mustering a gang of 80 men, we went ashore; and after picking up several stragglers, we surprized the *Lion*'s crew in the custom house just as they were about renewing their protections. We secured 17 of them, and guarding them along the streets, several hundreds of old men, women, and boys, flocked after us, well provided with stones and brickbats, and commenced a general attack; but not wishing to hurt them, we fired our pistols over their heads, in order to deter them from further outrage; but the women proved very daring, and followed us down to low water mark, being almost up to the knees in mud. We also pressed 16 men out of the *Nancy* and 14 out of the *Jenny*: the latter (being determine to preserve their liberty if possible) had confined their Captain and Chief Mate in order to fight their way through; and the Cook had got a pot full of boiling tallow to scald us with as we got up along side; but the wind being foul and not having a pilot, and the second Mate not daring to take charge of her in the river, they submitted to their fate. The *Ingrim* coming in from Turtola, we slipped, and following her into the Slyne, also pressed 26 of her men, whom Captain Nightingale ordered severally to the gang way for having fired into the tenders as they passed them at the rock.

Leaving Liverpool, we sailed to Douglas Bay in the Isle of Man, and thence to Dublin Bay, and after that to Plymouth, where we docked, and then were sent to convoy some victuallers to the grand fleet under the command of Admiral Hawke, Vice Admiral Hardy, and Commodore Young, who were blockading Brest harbour; and at our return, we were ordered by Commodore Hanway to convoy some more victuallers to Commodore Duff's squadron before Port L'Orient, and to join him. Here we lay at anchor as quietly as if we had been at Spithead, only we did not moor our ships, kept a better look out, and sometimes the Commodore would detatch part of the squadron to reconnoitre the coast, and keep a sharp look out at sea. Soon after this, being sent to cruise on the coast of Spain, in company with the *Firm* of 60 guns, the *Southampton* of 36, and the *Pallas* of 32, we were joined by the *Fortune* sloop of war of 14 guns, which was bound for England as a convoy to some light victuallers; but having the day before fallen in with the French grand fleet, commanded by Monsieur Conflans, she effected her escape by her swiftness of sailing, leaving the ships she had in charge to their fate, and proceeded to inform us of the fleet being out, and that it stood for Quiberon Bay. We were not surprized at this intelligence, as we had some nights before seen unusual lights on the coast of France. A council of war was now held on board the *Firm*, and it was agreed that the *Firm*, *Fortune*, and *Southampton*, should go in quest of the British fleet under the command of Sir Edward Hawke; the *Pallas* proceed to Cape Finisterre with intelligence for the Commanders of the *Fame* and *Winsor*, they being cruising off there; and the *Vengeance* endeavour to make Quiberon Bay, and, if possible, bring out the remainder of our squadron. Our Captain returning, we hoisted in our boat, and applied ourselves to the dangerous task assigned us, carrying a press of sail, all that night and the next day; and in the night of the 17th, we discovered ourselves almost in the midst of the enemy's fleet consisting of twenty-one sail of the line, and four frigates; but the wind blowing hard, and being very dark, we soon cleared them undiscovered, as they were on the contrary tack. The next day we saw them to leeward of us, but at such a distance that we thought ourselves in no danger; and on Monday the 19th, bringing the bay open, we made the signal to the squadron to cut or slip their cables, and come out with all possible speed, by which we effected the service we were sent out upon; and about two o'clock in the morning they joined us and having acquainted the Commodore with the cause of our alarm, we all stood close by the wind to the N. W. till four o'clock, when we tacked and stood to the southward, and at break of day we found ourselves but a small distance from the enemy; but they probably took us for the grand British fleet, which gave us an opportunity of making our escape; for while they were employed in clearing their ships, and forming a line of battle, we were making all the sail we could from them, and were quickly dispersed, each ship shifting for her own safety; and before they discovered their mistake, we had got a considerable distance; but they still gave us chase, and the *Thesee* of 74 guns was once within point blank musket shot of our ship, but did not fire at us, and by our superior alertness in setting and hauling down our steering sails, &c. repeatedly, as it blew very strong, and was squally, we got from her; but about ten o'clock in the forenoon, the *Portland* having sprung her main top-mast, was very near being taken; when the man at her fore top-mast head descried the English fleet, which the *Juno* had spoken with, coming to our relief under a press of sail, with a flown sheet, and the fore-tack at the cathead, on which the immediately hoisted her colours, and fired her stern chase-guns at the ship in chase of her, which alarming the French Admiral, he instantly made a signal for his fleet to collect and form a line of battle. The day now cleared up, and exhibited a grand and awful sight: – A powerful French fleet drawn up in fighting position, ready for action; and a British fleet with well appointed officers, and properly manned, bearing down upon it with crowded sail, and each breast glowing with ardor to decide the grand dispute betwixt the two nations, which should have the sovereignty of the seas. We now hoisted our colours, gave three cheers, took a reef in our top-sails, and hauling our wind, stood for the fleet, which we joined with gladness; and got our stream cable over the stern, ready to take a disabled ship in tow. But Conflans, on the near approach of our van, bore out of the line; and setting his fore-sail and topgallant-sails, led in shore; but seeing he was not followed by his Rear Admiral, he again shortened sail, and formed a regular line; but soon after, bearing away, let fall his fore-sail, loosed his topgallant-sails, and stood off. On which Admiral Hawke made the signal for a general chase, and for every ship to come to action as soon as she got up; and at fifteen minutes past two o'clock in the afternoon, Sir John Bentley, in the *Warspight* of 74 guns, being come alongside the *Formidable* of 80 guns, (their Rear Admiral's ship) the engagement commenced, but never became general, as the French kept leading away; by which means their van kept out of action; and many of the ships in our rear being far astern, could not get up; so that neither Admiral Hardy nor Commodore Young were able to come to action. When the *Warspight* had exchanged a few broad-sides, she shot ahead, and gave place to the *Revenge*, and she to *Dorsetshire*, &c. each ranging alongside the next ship in the enemy's rear; and the Admiral wishing to bring Conflans to engagement, weathered those ships which were in action, and ordered the Master of the *Royal George* to carry him alongside the *Soliel*: in assaying to do which he was intercepted by five sail of line of battle ships which he became engaged with all at once; but the *Superb* of 70 guns being fighting her lee guns, was taken in a squall, filled, and went down: A little after, the *Thesee* also sunk alongside the *Magnanime*, and the *Formidable* struck to the *Resolution*, which caused much confusion in the enemy's fleet. Not long after, the *Heroe* was disabled, and bore out of the line, but was followed by Lord Howe in the *Magnanime* of 76 guns, who ranged alongside of her; and the *Chatham* of 50 guns ran across her stern, and raked her: Thus sustaining the fire of both ships, she was at length obliged to strike, after having displayed the greatest bravery, and being almost reduced to a wreck. The *Formidable* too had suffered greatly, having received the fire of almost every British ship that came into action – the Admiral, most of her officers, and a great part of the crew, both seamen and mariners, being killed. Our boat took up four of the men belonging to the *Thesee*; the rest, together with all or most of the *Superb*'s crew, amounting to about 1615, perished. The ships going down in about fifteen fathoms depth of water, only their mast heads were to be seen; and we could perceive several of their dead men in the tops, and hanging amongst the shrouds and rigging. The French Admiral no doubt expected we should chase him; but as we were strangers to the coast, and might be without pilots, and night coming on, he led round the Cardinals, a range of rocks, which not appearing above water, are dangerous to mariners unacquainted with them; and the loss of many of our ships would probably have been the consequence of such a pursuit. But the British Admiral, perhaps aware of the danger, made a signal for his whole fleet to come to anchor, which was obeyed by all the ships except the *Resolution*, which kept under way, and the *Revenge*, *Defiance*, *Swiftsure*, and *Dorsetshire*, which having been disabled, had stood out to sea. The Captain of the *Resolution* being elated with success, gave his men an extra allowance of wine; and said he would stand off and on under an easy sail all night, and hoped to capture another of the French ships before the Admiral got his anchor up in the morning. About midnight we heard the firing of a gun, which kept being repeated, and which we considered as a signal of distress, but could not tell if it was an enemy's ship, or one of our own that was in danger. In the morning we discovered the cause, and had the mortification to see the *Resolution* on one of those rocks before mentioned, with her bottom out, all her masts gone, and her ensign reversed. On coming to anchor the preceding evening, our cutter took up 4 men from the wreck of the *Thesee*, by whom we were informed that the object of their expedition was to capture Commodore Duff's squadron, release the frigates he had blocked up in Port L'Orient, and then proceed with them to make a descent on the west of Ireland; but the gallant and swift-winged Hawke, who left Torbay the morning they sailed from Brest, happily prevented it. They also told us it was their Captain's intention to have ranged alongside the *Vengeance*; to have poured in a whole broad-side; and to have sent her to the bottom at once; for he had perceived she was French built, and that occasioned his chagrin; but the destruction he meditated against our ship fell to his own lot; for these 4 men and a few of the *Superb*'s were all that were saved

out of the two ships' crews. It blowing hard all night, the *Numur*
got under way to mend her birth, and came to again soon after; and
the *Soleil Royal*, which after it was dark, had come to anchor
betwixt us and the shore, cut her cable, and hoisting her jib, payed
round on her heel, let fall her fore-sail, and ran a-shore before the
wind, and was followed by the *Heroe*; on which the Admiral made
the signal for the *Essex* to chase them; but the Captain not being
aware of the extent of the rocks, and being wholly guided by his
lead, ran a-ground before he suspected the least danger, having had
twenty fathoms of water the cast before she struck. The *Maidstone*
and *Vengeance* being both under way, and standing for the
Resolution, on seeing the disaster which had be fallen the *Essex* (her
fore-mast having gone over her bow) immediately came to anchor,
and hoisting out our boats, we sent the cutter to assist the ships in
distress, and the barge to the *Formidable*, which had been kept possession of all the night by the midshipman and a cutter's crew; for
the men were so dispirited, they did not attempt to make the least
resistance, having had 300 killed, a much greater number
wounded, and the sides of the ship so shattered, that there was
scarcely a foot square of whole plank left from her head to her
stern. We then took some of the prisoners on board, and kept them
in our ship till we came home. Eight sail of the French line having
brought up under Penris Point, the signal was made for the whole
fleet to weigh and stretch under the land in quest of them. When
we were all under way, the Admiral made a signal to speak with
our Captain, when putting him on board the *Royal George*, he
ordered him to assist the *Portland* and *Chatham*'s boats in setting
fire to the two French ships that were a-shore, and which had been
abandoned by their crews. In effecting this service, we were considerably annoyed by a small battery on shore, but it did not prevent us
from completing our intended illumination. On the approach of
our fleet, the 8 French ships threw their guns over board, staved
their water-casks, and so far lightened them, that they got over the
bar into the river Vallaine, and having left their anchors ran a-shore
on the mud. A council of war being held, it was determined to burn
them if it could possibly be effected; and it was ordered that both
the launchs and long boats should all be converted into fire boats,
and sent amongst the ships; the whole to be conducted by Lord
Howe. In order to learn their position, the Admiral sent in a flag of

truce, under a pretence of complimenting them with the liberty of fetching a-shore the remains of their Rear Admiral, who was killed on board the *Formidable*, if they wished to have him interred. But the French having got their ships as far in as they could, and two 36 gun frigates being moored across the harbour's mouth, with springs on their cables, we found it impracticable to put our design in execution.

The men we saved from the wreck of the *Resolution*, told us, that some of their crew had attempted to save themselves by making a raft of some spars, and were driven out to sea; but we were afterwards informed, that on the return of the tide, they were thrown on shore, and made prisoners. The *Essex* and *Resolution* being both evacuated, we set fire to them on the 23d. day of November, to prevent them falling into the hands of the enemy; and having now performed the service we were sent out upon, and given a Coupe de Grace to the flower of the French fleet, Captain Campbell of the *Royal George*, came on board of our ship, charged with the Admiral's dispatches to the Lords Commissioners of the Admiralty, and we once more set sail for Old England.

Off Ushant, we fell in with Admiral Geary's fleet, and were hailed by the *Foudryant*, the Captain ordering us to bring to under the lee of the *Sandwich*, as the Admiral wanted to speak with us; but our Captain replied, that being charged with an express, he must not bring to; being asked what news, he answered Good News. We then made sail, and coming to Plymouth, landed the two Captains, and were then ordered off again; and should anybody ask us from whence we came, we were instructed to say from sea; and if they enquired what news? to say good news, and not to answer any further enquiries. However on our going on shore again in the evening, we found the intelligent west-country men knew almost as much of the affair as we did. The next day we put the prisoners on shore, and as soon as the wind was fair, we went up into Hamoaze, and then into dock; and were next sent to Cork. Whilst we lay there, the *Prince Edward* of Dublin, a vaunting Privateer, passed by; but shewing some insolence, we fired a gun athwart her forefoot, to bring her to, which not being regarded, we slipped, and followed her out to sea; and ranging along side of her, obliged her to comply; and a Lieutenant going on board, challenged 8 of her men as deserters from the navy, and took them out. We then returned to our anchors, and about a month after, took under convoy 7 sail of homeward-bound East India Men, and a Transport called the *Paddy and Jenny*, with recruits on board for the third or Plymouth division of marines; but being in want of seamen, I and five more were sent to assist the Captain in working her to Plymouth. When we got into a rough sea, the poor unseasoned recruits appeared like so many spectres; and when we came off the Lizard, we carried away our fore top-mast; but getting up a jury top-mast, top-sail yard, &c. and standing off shore (the wind being a-head) a recruit came forward, saying, Arah, where are we going? I told him to Plymouth. But, how, my dear joy, said he, can leaving the land be going to Plymouth? I said we should shortly put about and stand the other way, which joyful tidings he instantly communicated to his comrades, who all wished to be on land again, that they might have a little respite from the rough treatment they had already met with on the watery element. Having conducted them to Plymouth, we soon after sailed again to the eastward; and being off Portland, were overtaken with that very gale of wind which proved fatal to the *Ramelies* on the 6th of February 1760; and running through the Needles, brought up at Spithead; but going a-shore in the barge, we could not get off again for several days. After this, we went on several short channel cruises, in concert with the *Launceston*, with no other success than taking a few Privateers, Smugglers, &c. and docking at Portsmouth, we waited our sailing orders at Spithead. Soon after, the *Richmond* arrived there with an express from Lord Colville at Hallifax, informing Government that Quebec was closely besieged, if not taken. Whereupon we were ordered as soon as the despatches could be got ready, to take them on board, and proceed with them to Boston and Louisbourg, and also to Quebec if it had not surrendered. Putting to sea therefore with a foul wind, we beat down the channel, and arrived off Cape Breton in six weeks and three days, and after making the island, we lay to part of the night. The next day, there came on so thick a fog, that we could not see so far as our jib-boom end, so we fired a gun, which was answered from the sort whence we had been seen in the offing the day before: thus steering in by the report of their guns, we at length found ourselves embayed among the rocks; and having neither room to wear not stay, were obliged to drop our small bower-anchor under foot, and casting her head the other way, stood out again; and by the time we had got clear of the breakers, the *Thunderer's* boat (sent out on purpose to speak with us) dropped athwart our hawse, and informed us that Quebec was not taken; so delivering the dispatches consigned for Boston and Louisbourg to the Lieutenant, to be forwarded by Captain Proby to the Governors, &c. as they were directed, we instantly made sail for the Gulf of St Laurence; and at the isle of Beaque, took on board a pilot for the river; and arriving at Quebec, we found all safe and quiet; for as soon as the ice had broken up at Hallifax, the Commodore sailed with all the ships under his command to its relief; and sending the *Eurus* ahead to explore the state of the river, she proceeded as far as the isle of Beaque, and finding it full of loose ice, returned. The squadron keeping the sea ten days longer, entered the river with the *Eurus* and *Diana* in their van; and passing the isle of Orleans, and opening the town to view, they saw 3 French frigates a-breast of the Citadel, one of which had a broad pendant flying, and therefore supposed the place to be in the hands of the French; but as they could not return against wind and tide they hoisted their colours, and came to anchor; on which an English flag was hoisted at the fort; and the *Race-Horse* also, which had been frozen up below the town all the winter, hoisted her colours. The next day on the appearance of the *Vanguard*, *Northumberland*, *Prince of Orange*, and *Penzance* round the island, the French slipping their cables, ran up for the three rivers, and were then instantly chased by the two frigates, in which pursuit the *Diana* got on shore and was unfortunately lost: Captain Dean and his crew only being able to save the clothes on their backs. The army also on the back of the town, after spiking up the ordnance fled to Montreal; and General Murray leaving the government to Colonel Frazier, pursued them thither with his best troops, and being joined by General Amherst from Crown Point, and General Johnson from New York, they sat down before the place which afterwards surrendered; otherwise it must have shared the same fate as Quebec had done the year before, whilst it held out under the pressure of a long and powerful siege; for the forces against it were very powerful; and General Johnson had sent in a menacing summons, that if they refused to deliver it up, he would not restrain the indians he commanded, from exercising their wonted cruelty and barbarous ravages; which had such an effect upon the besieged that after some deliberation, they submitted to the terms proposed; and it was therefore immediately taken possession of by his Majesty's forces; and dispatches being prepared for Government we instantly received on board Major Berry charged with General Amherst's dispatches to the Secretary of State, and Commodore Colville's despatches to the Lords Commissioners of the Admiralty (intrusted to the care of Captain Dean, late of the *Diana* of 32 guns) we sailed with so much wind down the river that when we passed the isle of Coudre, the *Rochester*'s boat assayed to come along side with letters, but could not effect it (the ship running nearly 20 knots). We passed the Guard ship at Beaque in the night unnoticed. In the gulf the wind abating, and shifting to the eastward which was unfavourable, we had only light breezes till we made Cape Race in Newfoundland, where a gale at N. W. springing up in the first watch, brought us under our close-reefed top-sails and fore-course, and never could bear more sail till we saw the Land's End, which we did in 12 days, sometimes running 272, and never less than 240 miles a day, and coming to Portsmouth, we landed Major Berry and Captain Dean; after which an order came for us to dock; and we had not left the harbour when advice was received of his late Majesty's death; on which sad occasion we put all the ships into mourning, the mode of which is hoisting the colours $\frac{3}{4}$ staff up; but the next day, on the proclamation of his present Majesty's accession being made, we hoisted our colours quite up again, and conse-quently the formality of our mourning was at an end.

On coming out of Spithead, we were ordered by Vice Admiral Holbourn, to cruise in the channel between Portland and the Start; and taking a Smuggler off Sidmouth, we carried her into Plymouth which put us under the command of Rear Admiral Durel, who sometime after sent us to cruise off Ushant, and in the skirts of the Bay of Biscay; and being a little to the S. E. of the island, and standing in shore, we discovered breakers right ahead and on each bow, and being in the night, it caused great conster-nation amongst us: the Captain having taken the alarm, came upon deck in his shirt, and ordered the man at the wheel to put his helm a-weather; but the Master being more composed, signi-fied to the Captain, that not being room to wear the ship, there was no other way to extricate her out of danger, but by putting her helm a-lee, which was immediately done, and she came in stays, whereby we got into an open sea, and so were freed from our alarming apprehensions.

Cruising off Cape Pinus, we received intelligence of some vessels having sailed from Bourdeaux for Martinico; and shaping our course for them, in the middle watch of the night, between the 12th and 13th of March 1761, we espied a sail to which we gave chase, and in the morning perceived her to be a large sloop, and she having got us upon one mast, or right before the wind, by means of which our head-sails could not draw, she went from us; but seeing the *Orford* we made a signal for her to stop the chase, but she keeping her course too long before she tacked, was not able to render us any service; yet we continued our chase till 4 o'clock in the afternoon, when seeing no probability of coming up with her, and a large vessel appearing about four points on our larboard-bow, we altered our course and stood after her; and she being end on, and her mizzen top-sail furled, the officers who were observing with their glasses, conjectured she was a Dutch snow, as she did not make any sail from us, so that when the first dog-watch was out, the Captain ordered the hammocks down, and the watch below to get their suppers. About 8 o'clock I being on the fore-yard to keep sight of her, perceived her to set her mizzen top-sail, and lay it to the mast; so calling to the officer of the watch, I told him we came up very fast with the chase, which appeared to be a ship, and that she had loosed her mizzen top-sail, and laid it a-back. The Captain then ordered all hands to quarters, but to make no noise, nor cast any thing loose. When a youth, who could speak a little English, taking the trumpet, hailed us, saying, What ship is that? on which the Master in a low voice ordered us not to answer him, but to give him a gun, which he overhearing, said, Me be as ready as you; and instantly poured in a whole broadside, which killed and wounded several of our men and tore our mizzen top-sail to pieces, &c. Having cast loose our guns, we returned their compliment, and then sheered off to bend another top-sail, and clear and barricade the ship. Being now prepared, we again made sail after her, sustaining the fire from her stern chase-guns as we approached her for a considerable time; but having got sufficiently near, and ranging alongside, we renewed the engagement with vigor, which they as smartly returned, and were so near us, that (although we had the weather-gage) their wads fell on our quarter deck, and catching the loose powder, set our ship on fire five times, and communicating to some cartridges, (which the boys through their eagerness had brought up faster than they were wanted) blew up, and wounded five of our marines. They had the advantage of us by being furnished with star-shot, sliding-shot, double-head, langridge, &c. which tore our sails and running rigging to pieces; whilst we had only round, grape, and double head in return; however, such means as we had in our power, we made so good an use of, that they seemed anxious to decline the contest; and putting their helm hard a-lee, and luffing up, endeavoured to run on board of us betwixt our main and mizzen chains; but our ship answering her weather-helm, it was prevented, and they dropping a-stern, shot up a windward of us, and we stood to our weather guns. In the heat of the action, their ensign staff being shot away, we supposed they had struck, and accordingly gave them three cheers; but they renewing the action, we instantly did the same; but though they had gained the wind, they soon after ceased firing; yet kept a flag flying at the mizzen top-mast head; for they found it impossible to get it down, on account of their mizzen mast being so much shattered. Our master then hailing, asked if they had struck; to which it was answered, Me no fightee no more; send your boat and see. The question was repeated, and the same answer returned. They then asked what ship ours was; we said the *Phenix* of 40 guns. They then told us to send our boats; but our lists, braces, yard-tackles, &c. being shot away, instead of hoisting out the boat, we were obliged to watch a lee-lurch of the ship, and launch the cutter overboard; and coming alongside their vessel, the French Captain, standing in the main chains, stepped in, saying, put off, for the ship is sinking. When he got on board our ship, and found her to be the *Vengeance*, he exclaimed, O Sacra Dieu! O foutue frigate. We found her much shattered, with several holes between wind and water, and seven feet of water in the hold, and her sails, masts, and rigging almost cut to pieces. She was called *Le Enterprenant*, and had been a Malteese ship of war of 50 guns; but was now a French Letter-of-Marque, mounting 6 eighteen-pounders, and 20 nine-pounders, having 203 men, of whom 16 were killed and 23 wounded in the action; and on our side, the sail-maker, 3 seamen, and a marines were killed; and the master, 2 midshipmen, a quartermaster, the gunner's mate, 14 seamen, and 7 marines wounded. Mr Sebit, the gunner's mate, and 3 more died of their wounds. Mr George Noble, midshipman, had his left hand, and part of his right, shot off, and received a musket-ball through the thick part of both his thighs, but still recovered, and was afterwards made a Lieutenant. Christopher Carling, the quartermaster, also recovered of a wound he received in the shoulder, which rendered it necessary to have the blade bone extracted, which was done by several severe operations, and taken out piece by piece. When we had removed the prisoners, and put an officer and men on board the prize, we began to knot and splice our rigging, bend new sails, stop leaks, and repair other damages we had sustained in the engagement; and having now more French than English on board our ship, it became necessary to be upon our guard; wherefore we always slept under arms, having a cartouch-box belted on, and a loaded pistol and a cutlass ready, sleeping on the deck instead of below, as it alternately became our turn, being wrapped up in some spare sails; and we also kept sentinals at the hatchways, and had blunderbusses on the combings, ready to fire amongst the prisoners, if necessary; and this vigilance we were obliged to continue till we arrived in port.

After taking possession of the prize, and removing the prisoners, it came on to blow very hard, and we were thereby exposed to the danger of loseing both ships on a lee shore, which was an enemy's coast; for though our own ship was pretty well equipped, yet the prize had lost both her mizzenmast and fore top-mast (which went over the side soon after she struck) and her main-mast being wounded, she could not for some time set a stitch of sail; which made us think of taking the hands out, and letting her sink; in order to which we hoisted out our cutter; but finding she could not live in such a high sea, we hoisted her in again; and the men having secured the main-mast, got up a jury top-mast, and repaired the rigging, set the courses, top-sails, and some stay-sails; and when the gale abated, we took her in tow. Off Ushant we saw a large ship bearing down on our weather-beam, which animated the prisoners almost to mutiny; but on her hoisting English colours, and hailing us, they became silent. When we were a-breast of the Lizzard, the hauser broke, so (the wind being at S. W. by W.) we left the prize, and made sail to speak with a vessel we saw crouding away from a Ketch that was in chase of her; and coming up, and firing a musket, brought her to, then joined our other prize, and took them both into Plymouth sound together.

After that, our ship going up into Hamoaze, was there surveyed; and on such survey being deemed unfit for future service, was accordingly laid up at moorings as a hulk. And the *Winchester* of 50 guns having had a thorough repair, and being in want of hands, we were turned over to her, and sent to the Downs to join Sir Piercy Brett's squadron, and receive on board Captain John Dalrymple from the *Solebay*, he being appointed to command us. Where having continued some time, orders came for us and the *Nottingham* to weigh, and proceed to Osley-bay, and there join Lord George Anson, Admiral of England, who hoisted the union flag on board the *Royal Charlotte*; and on the 8th of August, we sailed from thence for Hamburg, where we arrived in a few days, and the *Nottingham* and *Winchester* brought up at the red-bouy within Halygalanht, the *Tartar* at some distance higher up, and the *Minerva*, &c. went quite to Cruxhaven, where they waited for the arrival of her Royal Highness Princess Charlotte of Mechlenberg, then by proxy, Queen of Great Britain. When she and her attendants were embarked, on the display of a signal, which was repeated by the *Tartar*, we took up our anchors and laid to, till we were joined, on which the Admiral's flag was shifted to the *Nottingham*, and the royal standard being displayed at the Yacht's mast head, each ship saluted her Majesty with 21 guns, and made sail. His lordship having given orders for the purpose, we were obliged strictly to observe them in sailing, viz. the *Hazard* of 8 guns to keep in the van, at two miles distance, to look out; the *Tartar* of 28 guns also a-head, at one mile distance; the *Nottingham* of 60 guns, on her starboard-beam, and the *Winchester* of 50 guns, on her larboard-beam, each at two cable lengths distance; also the *Minerva* of 32 guns, as far a-stern as the *Tartar* was a-head; and the *Lynx* of 14 guns, likewise in the rear, at two miles distance; and with her the *Mary, Augusta, Fubbs, William and Mary* Yachts, and a store-ship. The Reverend Dr Croker being asked his opinion respecting the weather, said, the appearance of the heavens portended a pleasant voyage. But it soon after began to blow very hard, which continued for several days; and the wind veering to the southward, we were apprehensive we should be obliged to land our Mistress either at Hull or Grimsby; but it coming fair, we arrived safe off Harwich,

September 6, in the afternoon, and again firing a royal salute, parted company; and leaving the *Minerva* and *Lynx* to go in with the Yachts, we, with the *Nottingham*, *Tartar*, and *Hazard*, bore away for the Downs, where we stayed till orders came for our ship to proceed to Portsmouth, there to dock, sheath and fill, for foreign service.

Having completed our stores and provisions, got our guns in, &c. we went out of harbour; and after waiting at Spithead a few days, orders came for us to sail for the coast of Guinea, and from thence to the West Indies, but to touch at Plymouth in our way, where Captain Nightingale had got command of the *Flora* frigate of 32 guns, and who, on our arrival, produced an order of the admiralty to demand 40 of those men from the *Winchester* which had sailed with him in the *Vengeance*; when we being called aft, Captain Dalrymple chose one, and Lieutenant Hawker of the *Flora* another, until he had obtained his number, in which I was included, and went with him on board the frigate, (which had been taken by the *Unicorn*, and her name changed from that of *Vestal*) she being very far short of her complement, and many petty offices vacant, to which several were advanced who I was confident were neither so good seamen, nor of so long duration in the service as myself, by which I thought I was neglected and much injured. Mr Hawker too being now first Lieutenant, and having gained an ascendency over the Captain's temper, seemed more haughty in his station than formerly, which with some other concurrent circumstances, made me take my land-tacks on board; wherefore on going ashore, I bought myself some long clothes, and changing my habit, gave away my jackets, shirt, trowsers, and shoes, set off on horseback to Exeter, where I discharged my attendants and went down to Topsom, and agreed with the Master of a Snow bound to Lisbon and from thence to Charles Town in South Carolina; but not liking the vessel, I set off on foot for London, and as I was entering into the town of Honiton, an old woman met me, saying, young man, are you afraid of the soldiers? I said no, mother, and walked boldly up the street past them as they were parading. When I came at Axminster, I found a return-chaise to Bridport, and next morning proceeded to Dorchester by the same mode of conveyance. From thence I walked to Blandford, and next to Salisbury, and down to Peterfinger, where taking the wagon, I came to Southampton before day-light. I next walked to Gosport, and crossing the water to Portsmouth, took an inside place in the coach at the Red Lion, from whence I set off about 3 o'clock, in company with a young Lieutenant appointed for the *Alarm* frigate, (then lying at Woolwich, on which an experiment of copper-sheathing was making) a young midshipman belonging to the *Portland*, and a lady and child who belonged to a Lieutenant of the said ship; I durst not seem afraid of my company, so we entered on agreeable conversation; and when we came at Portsdown bridge, the Sergeant of the guard opened the coach door, saying, have you any seamen here? to which the Lieutenant (who was dressed in uniform) said no; the Sergeant said, Oh, sir, I take your word; so we drove on to Petersfield, where we breakfasted. Here the Lieutenant proposed our bearing the lady free of expence on the road till we came to Town, to which I readily consented, being always willing to oblige the fair sex whenever it lay in my power. As we passed through a grass field, the gentleman asked me what it was worth? taking me, I suppose, either for a surveyor, owner or occupier of land: I said, in order to give a proper estimate, it would be necessary to alight, walk round it, examine the soil, and make an admeasurement, and then determine its value. Sometimes he would address himself to the midshipman about ships and naval tactics, about which I dared not to say a word, lest I should betray myself by using some sea-phrase or other; so I affected to be the rustic countryman they supposed me to be, observing silence, and never interrupting them. We dined at an old house before we came at Godalming, and only one table being provided, all sat down together. Among the outside passengers was one in livery; this circumstance was so disgustful to the Lieutenant, that it saved much of the landlord's meat, by spoiling his stomach, so that we conceived he was not well; but as the waiter was serving up the wine, he made his objection, saying, that scoundrel shall not drink with me! on which the servant said, Sir, if my presence be disagreeable, I'll withdraw; and calling for some rum and water, retired into another room. When we were again on the road, the gentleman said to me, Sir, did you not observe the insolent behaviour of that fellow in livery at the inn? I wonder at his impudence, to sit down to table with us. I said, Sir, I never mind such trifles; the man wanted refreshment, and had no more time, you know, than we, and therefore was not to blame; it was the landlord's fault in not providing two tables for the passengers. He said, Oh, sir, I beg your pardon; he ought to have known better; had it been a common sailor or soldier, I should not have minded; but a livery servant ought to know good manners; perhaps to-morrow I may dine with his master, and he wait at table: I suppose those two chaps introduced him (meaning two outside passengers who some-times rode inside) but they shall not drink tea with us, we'll keep to ourselves, and have nothing to do with those outsides. So arriving at Guildford, we accordingly had a room to ourselves, where we drank tea; but here I was guilty of a small offence against the gen-tleman's feelings; for a pretty girl having waited on us, I made her a present of a shilling for which she made me a very fine courtesy; he thought it extravagant, and told me I gave in too courtly a stile; he thought six-pence a piece would have been plenty; to which I replied, sir, the maid took my fancy, but my example laid no obli-gation on any other person. When we approached near Kennington common, we became very anxious for the safety of our money, in case of meeting with a collector on the road, as it began to be dark; so I put mine into my glove, and concealed it in a hole I found in the lining of the coach roof; and the gentlemen gave theirs to the lady, who sewed it, together with her own, in the border of her pet-ticoat, each of us reserving a few shillings to satisfy a needy gentleman who might suddenly start from behind a gibbet post and make a demand.

We arrived safe at the Spread Eagle in Grace-Church Street about 8 o'clock, where my travelling companions calling hackney coaches to convey them to their respective friends' houses, left me; and I knowing nobody in London, stayed all night at the inn, and next morning set off to Deptford to seek a ship; and finding one bound to Guadalope, I shipped myself to go in her for 2l. 15s. per month, and left her the next day to go on board the *Elizabeth* East Indiaman, commanded by Captain George Stuart, bound to Bencoolen and China. Mr Abraham Sheppey, 1ft. Mr William Ayres, 2nd. Mr Peter Bearsley, 3rd. Mr Paine Voice, 4th. Mr Francis Gillow, 5th. and Mr John Morgan, 6th. Mate, for only 2l. 5s. per month, being the most given in the India service. When I had got my chest and bedding down between decks, it became necessary to put off my long-lapped coat, and array myself in the proper badges of my profession, which being all new, the men said they had got

quite a new sailor from slop-shop, but were soon convinced of their
mistake. When we had took in a considerable part of our cargo, we
dropped down to Gravesend to complete it, and take in our guns
(26 nine-pounders) together with our stores and provisions, and
received 30 company's soldiers on board from Blackwood's office
on Tower-Hill. These poor fellows are generally kidnapped and
kept in certain offices till the ships are at Gravesend, whether they
are sent, and kept under a guard until they sail. The company allow
each man 5l. bounty, which is laid out for necessaries, and the sur-
plus, if any, given them; but they have no pay till they arrive in
India, when they enter on nine rupees a month, which is equal to 1l.
2s. 6d. of our money. So soon as we could be spared from work, I
and some more men were sent up to meet the Captain at the India-
House in Leadenhall street, and receive our impress-money, viz.
two months pay, and impower an agent to receive a like sum in our
behalf, when the Directors had received advice of our safe arrival in
the country. We were ordered to keep in our lodgings, as the protection was not of force without an officer attending, but I did not
adhere to this order; and one day as I stood at a book-stall on Little
Tower-Hill, Mr Richard Thomas, late first Lieutenant of the
Vengeance, came and looked at some books, then at me, and I at
him, yet neither of us spoke; nor durst I go till he was gone, he
never before having seen me in long clothes, I supposed he did not
know me. I met him again another day in East Smith-field with a
press-gang in his rear.

On the 4th of January, 1762, I went to meet the procession, and
hear war against Spain declared, by Mr Molineaux, king at arms,
and met it in the Strand advancing to Temple-bar, which gate was
shut on the occasion, and the Lord Mayor in waiting on the city side
in his mayoral coach till the Herald should ask leave for entrance
into the city. The sight was awfully grand: In van was two life-
guard-men, each with a battle-axe in his hand, and his arm
extended; these were followed by several files of life-guards preceding the Herald, who was followed by four other Heralds; and in
their rear many more files of life-guards closed the cavalcade,
which was again followed by a numerous train of coaches, and people on foot; also the top of the gate-way, as well as the roofs and
windows of the houses, were crowded with spectators. As the van
advanced, they faced to the left, and with extended arm presented

themselves against the wall; the other files closed in their rear to make way, when the Herald advancing up to the gate, requested admission into the city, in his Majesty's name: At the third request, the gates were opened, and the procession advancing through, halted, when Mr Molineaux read the declaration to the gaping audience, every one wishing to hear and know the political reasons of such declarations. It was repeated at the royal exchange and again at the bridge foot, where the scene closed.

Having completed our business at Gravesend, we fell down into the Hope; and next day, February 2, received our river-pay; and three days after, his Majesty's ship, *Blenheim*, coming down the reach, carried away her main and fore-top masts, which accident obliged her to bring up; and while she remained by us, a Lieutenant came on board and mustered our hands, saying, he had received information of some deserters. While we lay here, advice was received of the capture of Bencoolen by Commodore de Estang, on which we were ordered to unlade the goods consigned for it, and the soldiers were removed to the *Winchelsea*, commanded by the honourable Thomas Howe, bound to Bombay; so that keeping only about 600 tons of flint, some iron, a small quantity of Dorchester beer, some casks of quicksilver, and 17 chests of dollars, on board, the ship was little more than half loaded: She, together with the *Harcourt* and *Orson*, were directed to China only. On leaving the river, we proceeded across the flats, and (none of us being acquainted with the ship, as she was new) by venturing too near before we put her in stays, and as she kept shooting a-head while she was coming about, she went a-ground on Margate sands, where we lay a whole tide, and were all hands at work in unstowing the spars, and shouring her up, lest she should settle on her bulge, as the tide fell; and carried out the stream-anchor a-stern in the boat, in order to heave her off as she began to float with the rising tide; (it snowing all the night, though the wind was moderate) so getting her afloat at half flood, we stretched round the foreland, and came into the Downs, where we rode out that severe storm in which so many perished by the inclemency of the weather in Lincolnshire and other parts of the kingdom. Here Mr Sheppey died, on which occasion we put the ship into mourning, and his corpse being landed at Deal, was attended with such naval honours as were due to his station in the service.

Before we left the Downs, the *Flora* came round from Sheerness, and brought up within three cable lengths of us; however when the other ships from the river had joined us, we sailed under convoy (or rather, direction) of a sloop of war, and arrived at Spithead, where Admirals Pecocke and Keppel lay bound on an expedition against Havannah. While we lay here, Mr Thomas Thomas, appointed Super-cargo, and Mr John Matthews, Chief Mate, came over-land to us; and on the 25th of March, we broke ground and put to sea, in company with the *Prince Henry, Royal Charlotte, Clinton, Hardwick, Orson*, and *Harcourt*, under convoy of his Majesty's ships *Arrogant*, Captain Amherst, of 74, and *Royal William*, Captain Pigot, of 84 guns, but did not clear the land before the 1st of April, when we took our departure from Cape Cornwall, and the same day lost a man as we were about to reef out top-sails.

We soon got into a warm climate, and on arriving in the vicinity of the Canaries, Captain Amherst made the signal for separation, and he and the other ship of war bore up or hauled their wind, leaving us to the conduct of Captain Henry Best of the *Prince Henry*, who was senior Captain in the service, and who now became Commodore of the fleet. Some time after, we parted company with all our consorts except the *Hardwick* and *Harcourt*, and crossed the line on the 9th of May, and were called on for our bottle and pound; and as many of us had never before been in the southern hemisphere, it made us plenty of punch. Here, as we were sometimes becalmed, and the rains fell very heavy, we filled many of our empty casks with water, which served our live stock and fowls, and spared our river water for our own use, which we obtained by boreing holes in the water-courses of the upper deck, and when the rain had washed it clean, we stopped the scuppers, then fixed a hose or pipe made of sail canvass to one of these, leading it down the hatchway, placed the small end in the bung-hole of a cask till it was full, and then shifted it into another. We also caught a good deal of fish.

When we had got into the south east trade, we rigged out our out-riggers; and with strong pendants well set up, so strengthened our rigging and secured our lower mast, as to enable us to carry a press of sail and run with a flown sheet, and the fore-tack just before the cat-head, in order the sooner to get into a variable wind's way, meaning to make the island of Trinidada on the coast of South

America, but missed it in the night; and arriving in latitude 28, 45, where we gained a fair wind at W. N. W. we shaped our course for the Cape of Good Hope, and as we approached it, saw many of those birds known by the names of cape hens and albatrosses, which fly about at some distance from it: The former of these resemble a guinea-hen, and the latter are of an enormous size; the wings of some of them, when expanded, are from seven to nine feet in extent; we used to say they were old transmigrated pursers, &c. We also caught some fine dolphins, albacores, and bonettas, which are excellent fish. Arriving off the cape on the 20th of June, the wind at S. W. very cold, accompanied with snow, we hove to to sound, when the *Hardwick* got ground in 97 fathoms depth of water, and making the signal, we each filled our sails and stood on. This sounding served the purpose of correcting our reckoning as much as though we had seen the land.

After we had doubled Cape Falsa, Captain Sampson took his leave of us, steering a more northerly course, as he meant to touch at Johanna, or Cochin, for wood and water, in his way to Bengal, while we and the *Harcourt* edged away more to the southward, till we had raised our latitude to about 39 degrees; then running our longitude, intended to fall in with one of the little islands of Amsterdam or Saint Paul, and take a fresh departure from it, but missed them both. Our ship being a prime sailer, we were able to run under a comparative small sail all the way through this stormy sea, while the *Harcourt*, our consort, carried a press of canvass to keep up with us, Captain Murray shewing great anxiety to avoid a separation; however soon after we had found ourselves to the east-ward of the afore-mentioned islands, and thereupon altered our course, we lost sight of her in the course of the night; and steering again across the S. E. trade, stood for Java Head, which we discov-ered at some distance on our starboard beam, and came to anchor under Cockatore island, in the streights of Sonda, in the evening of the 27th of July, after having been out of sight of land 119 days, including those of our departure and land-fall, in which time we had run a distance of 4000 leagues, due course; and, including our various traverses, a much greater. The next day we weighed, stood further up the streights, and brought up again under one of the Brothers (three little islands so called) and the day following manned the yawl and went ashore on the island of Sumatra, but

without arms, left we should give any alarm to the natives, of
whom we obtained intelligence where to get a supply of wood and
water. We landed in a small creek, where we found several proas,
i.e. small vessels, with sails made of matting; and on the shores, a
quantity of wigwams or huts, built of bamboos and kajan, in and
about which were several men and boys armed with each a crest,
i.e. a kind of short scimetar, which by its colour appeared to have
been touched with the gum of upas; but we saw neither women nor
children, yet concluded they had concealed them at our approach,
as also their cattle, for we discerned fresh dung, and the impression
of buffaloes' feet, &c. on the beach: I suppose they thought our principal design might be on one of those articles, if we came with any
hostile intention; but convinced of the contrary by our peaceable
demeanour, they were very civil, and took our trinkets in exchange
for oranges, melons, paroquets, &c. and so parting with them in
friendship, we returned to the ship. My messmate, whose name was
Steward Gray, having formed a design previous to his shipping
himself in London, mentioned it to me and two more of the boats'
crew, William Oliver and Robert Sims (when each of us unhappily
fell into his scheme without due consideration of its nature and ten-
dency) and having been employed in landing some of the sick on
one of the brothers, made an excuse of going to leeward of the
island, as though we intended to shoot birds; but when we were out
of view, set the sails, having only a little bread and a small keg of
water, with 3 muskets and 3 cutlasses in the boat; each of us leaving
four months pay behind; and I for my own part, a chest of clothes,
bedding, and books, which cost me above eighteen pounds in
England. We ran about three leagues down the streights, and then
stretched over to the Java shore; and when the sea-breeze died
away, we rowed; but next day our water being exhausted, and the
heat at noon, under an almost vertical sun, intense, a debate was
entered into about getting a supply, as some were fearful of venturing ashore; but on getting sight of some huts near the beach, I said
we had as good perish by the hands of the natives as by thirst; so we
pulled in, and put ashore; and leaving Sims in the boat, ascended
the beach, advanced to one of the wigwams with our empty keg,
and made signs that we wanted water; on which they favoured
each of us with a draught. We then signified that we wanted some
in our keg, when a Malay man made signs for one of us to follow

him with it, which Steward Gray readily consented to. They went into a mangrove behind a spacious mansion, a little detached from the shore; and some time after they were out of sight, our ears were alarmed with a hideous yelling, which seemed to issue out of the grove, which alarming our fears for the safety of our companion, we had some thoughts of arming ourselves and going to seek him; but considering the weakness of our party, did not attempt it. We entered into conversation with an old Malay, who spoke some Dutch, from whom we learned how Batavia bore off us, and how far distant it was from us. Our fears exciting watchfulness, with wishful eyes we often looked toward the grove, and at length saw Gray and his guide coming down to the beach. When they had joined us, Gray told us he had been bartering for some melons and bananas; so taking leave of our friends, we put off, and steering athwart Bantam bay, shaped our course according to the old man's direction. And on making the land again at night, fell into a current setting from the land, the water of which was very white, thick, and muddy, near the surface, but very fresh and palatable: On dividing it, and taking some up a little deeper, it was clearer, but brackish; and on plunging a bamboo about three feet deep, we found it perfectly clear, and as salt as it is out at sea. About two o'clock in the morning, we came under a small flat island, where hooking a porous stone, we fastened the boat's painter to it, and rode by it as an anchor till day-light, two of us watching and two sleeping; then casting loose, we rowed for another island, which proved to be Ondross; and passing it, got a full view of Batavia, and in the road, four sail of French ships of the line, but not one English vessel; which was a mortifying circumstance to us, as we had the day before seen one in the Offing, which we here learned was gone for Madras, though our intent was to have procured a passage to Calcutta, and there engage in country ships, which are trading vessels navigated by lascars, with only a white Captain, Boatswain, and Gunner, who are allowed a stipulated quantity of property on board, as private trade or venture, in augmentation of their wages, which presented us with a view of accumulating fortunes and being great.

We arrived at Batavia about 10 o'clock on the 4th of August, and some time elapsed without any prospect of accomplishing our wishes, in a strange and sickly country, out of any kind of employment, our boat gone, and our money well nigh exhausted. We at length applied to the Dutch Commodore, Mynheer Rosiboom, with whom we shipped ourselves, on condition of being sent home in the sygar schips which were to sail for Europe the latter end of October, and were sent on board of an old ship called the *Spaarsimaaht*, in the road, where Gray and Oliver being taken ill, were sent ashore to the sick hoyse or hospital.

Soon after this, the *Orson* having arrived in the streights, seven of her men came after us in the pinnace, which the Dutch Commodore seized; but four of the men shipped themselves immediately with one Captain Jackson, an Englishman, who commanded a Portugues brigg, bound to Macoa, and sailed the next day; and the other three came into the same employ as we were in, and the Commodore sent them also on board the guard-ship. The sygar schips beginning to take in their cargoes, the Commodore came on board and ordered me and Jeremiah Painter to the *Livdee*, and the other three to the *Oude frou Elisabet*, which we respectively assisted to load with the rich produce of their fruitful colonies; and when they were almost ready for sea, he came again to see how they were manned; so the hands being called to muster, we appeared on the quarter-deck, and the steerman said, Mynheer, heer bene de Englesmen; he said, yaw, let dem neer geloupen: So we went to work again unconcerned; but one of the bargemen came and said to me, Yack, ga yie de hoyce to; I said, yaw; to which he answered, dat wit ich neet; which words gave me a strong suspicion: And at night as I lay asleep on a chest under the half-deck with Jerry on the deck by me, a lad came and awoke me, saying, Yark, de steerman roopt yie de halefdeck op; so I said, come, Jerry, let us go aft; when espying the long-boat along side, I said, we are sold, but never mind, my lad; for I knew it was the boat that carried transports to some of the islands. The Mate said, Englesmen! yie muht yire keft ant gooht gecragen, op an andor schip muht yie wesen. I said, Mynheer, bene de and or schip gaing de fador lanht to; he said, ich wit it neet, tou gou: So getting our chest and bedding into the boat, we put off and stood away before the land-breeze; and looking at the compass, and seeing we steered E. N. E. I said, where are we going? the quarter-master said, on the wall; I said, where to? he answered, to Batavia; I again said, nay, ich wit fel beeter; adding, I believe we are going to some island to be made slaves; he said, nay, we were going to an island, but not to be slaves; at which I exclaimed, a pack of thieves! what have we done to be so dealt with? he said it was the Commodore's order, in consequence of having received intelligence of some English man of war being in the streights, which he supposed would take us away from them, and that we should be fetched back when it was known that she was gone. I said we are seamen and know not how to work ashore; why did he not send us to some other place where the trading ships were going? About 3 o'clock in the morning, October 23, we arrived at a jetty, and remained in the boat till 5, when we were ordered to land our things and carry them into a shed, much like a barn, which was to be our habitation, then go drink a soupy, and go to work. The name of the island is Edam, lying E. N. E. from Batavia, distant 6 leagues, whither they send such criminals as are not deemed worthy of death, some of whom are sentenced to 3 months' confinement, others to 6 months, 9 months, 1 year, 2 years, 3 years, 7 years, 10 years, 15 years, 25 years, and some 99 years, in proportion to the nature and degree of their offences, or the compassion or implacability of their judges.

Three days after, the other three men were taken from the *Oude frou Elisabet* and brought to bear us company and take their lot amongst us, but Oliver was removed from the hospital on board a ship bound to Japan, and Gray coming out when the fleet was on the point of sailing, was put on board a ship bound to Rotterdam; and, when I came to London in 1766, was Chief Mate of a ship then lying in the pool, bound to the West Indies; so that he who brought us into the snare, fared the best. Our employment in this airy prison was mostly that of making cables and cordage of caiau or the fibres of cocoa-nut husks, or twice laid stuff, i.e. cordage made of old hawsers and cables cut into lengths, opened out, and the yarns dressed, knotted, laid over again, and tarred. But when we had not sufficient to keep us employed, we were set to gather stones, or wheel sand and gravel into the tyne, or garden, which was spacious, and well planted with fruit-trees, plants, flowers, and herbs; and at leisure opportunities to rake up the fallen leaves and burn them. Our labour was by no means hard, as we generally rose about 5 o'clock and went to kirk, then drank a soupy or dram of arrack, went to work at 6, left for breakfast at 8 and were allowed half an hour; left for dinner at 12 and went to work again at 1, left at 5 and

went to kirk, received another dram at 6; and we, with a number of
youths who were nominated frie-youngers, had alternately to keep
watch during the night, at the prisons and other posts once every
other night. In one of these prisons was kept the white banditti,
consisting of Dutch, English, Danes, French, &c. amongst whom
were some Moors, who were baptized; and in the other were confined the Pagan Moors, Malays, Gentoos, and other blacks: Here
the boys would sometimes fancy they saw ghosts and apparitions,
and affrighted themselves from their posts. But our provisions were
scanty and unwholesome; as a substitute for bread, we had rice
boiled as dry as possible; and as to animal food, we had, on
Sundays, a small allowance of fresh pork, the fat of which was as
purgative as jalap, by reason of the hogs eating a kind of fruit called
cattatas, which grow there in plenty, and fall off the trees; on
Tuesdays, either a small piece of salt beef which had been sometimes four or five years in the cask, or a small portion of schelpat or
tortoise, which was the best meal we ever got; and on Thursdays, a
small quantity of salt pork, which had been dried in the smoke in
Holland and was quite rotten with age: – Those were our meat-
days; and on the four banian days, as follows, viz. on Mondays and
Wednesdays we were served with a little salt-fish, which was sometimes so rotten that it would not hold together: On Fridays we had
a sort of gruel made of rice, with tamarinds and molasses, which
they called grub-yack; and on Saturdays, another kind of gruel
qualified with sugar and cocoa-nut milk (the nut being scraped and
infused in water and then strained) this they called lip-lap. I have
been thus particular that the reader may have an idea how some
people live; but as we frie-youngers had wages, we could sometimes
get a bit of fresh fish, for the company allowed any fisherman rice
for his family's use that might bring fish to the island; and boats
came from Batavia with fish and eggs, ready cooked; fruits, yams,
sweet potatoes, and sometimes bread; and Captain Swaarht, our
governor, for a while, kept a cook's shop.

This little isle is about a mile in circumference, with a flat
surface, very little raised above the level of the sea, great part of it
covered with trees and copswood, among which run a number of
deer and some sheep; and the ground being nitrous, rendered it
exceedingly unhealthful, subjecting us to fevers, blotches, &c. which
caused frequent instances of mortality. In February, one of my

ship-mates was taken ill, and in a few days after, two more of them, all of whom died before lady-day, leaving only me and Jeremiah Painter, who also died, and I attended him to his long home on the 13th of May; so that being now bereft of my companions, I had a good opportunity to acquire much of the Dutch language; but my situation brought a kind of gloominess on my mind, and rendered the learning a new tongue rather more irksome than delightful, and bent my thoughts on devising means for escape, in order to which, I at leisure times, gathered some bamboos on the back of the island, and provided some cordage which I deposited in a bush, intending to make a raft; I also procured an oar to steer with, meaning to make a sail of my large hammock; and, when the monsoons would permit, put off in the night with a strong easterly wind, and make the Java shore, there get amongst the Malays, and abide with them till some English ship should arrive, determined rather to perish in such an attempt, than stay where I was. However before I could put this scheme in practice, the Quarter-master of the long-boat (who was a Dane and spoke English, with whom I had often conversed) took me with him to Batavia, where staying three days, I sought for the English Consul, resident there, who could have released me, being a British subject, but I found only the Clerk, who told me his Master was gone to Bencoolen. Of this gentleman I learned the fate of my ship, *Elizabeth*, and afterwards obtained a more accurate account of her catastrophe from Mr John Ogelby, a Midshipman on board of her at that time, whom I met with at the Cape of Good Hope, and who then belonged to an outward-bound ship commanded by Mr Henry Gardener, late our purser. He said, the ship having completed her cargo at Wampoa, had dropped down and joined the homeward bound ships at Macoa, and while she lay there, a Dutchman, who was her sail-maker, having got drunk, after the crew was gone to sleep let a candle fall amongst some oakum, which taking fire, communicated to the pitch of the seams which were calked and payed, but not scraped, and ran along them to the cables, the smoke of which suffocating the men who slept in the cable tiers, their cries alarmed those that lay on the gun-deck, who used their utmost efforts to extricate them from then dreadful situation, and save the ship from destruction, but without effect; and several who were exerting themselves in a fruitless endeavour to rescue their fellows from death, shared the same fate:

Amongst these heroes were Mr Bearsley and Mr Gillow, two fine young fellows who perished from a pure principle of philanthropy. At length the flames rapidly spreading fore and aft, the ship became an entire conflagration; and burning down to the water's edge, the bottom sunk. – Thus perished one of the finest ships that ever crossed the Indian ocean, with a cargo worth near half a million, and thirty-six precious lives, (including Captain Stuart, who refused to quit her) through the carelessness and stupidity of an individual, who instead of giving the necessary alarm, had secretly escaped from the ship to secure himself, without shewing any concern for the rest. How dear is life! a man whose name was Andrew Seaton during the awful scene, got over-board and caught hold of the rudder-rings where he supported himself till several holes were burnt in his head, before a boat came to take him away, not daring to quit his hold because he could not swim. But to return; hoping a more favourable opportunity for effecting my escape might occur, I returned with the boat, and as some of the men were employed in cleaning the arms, they formed a scheme to seize her and run to Bencoolen, but their plot being discovered, the principal conspirator was confined to live on congee for a fortnight, to run the gantelope. When a black died on the island, he was interred with the burial of an ass; when a christian convict died, he was attended to the grave by those of his own class; and when a frie-younger died, he was attended by such as bore that character; the clergymen never attended at any of these funerals; and those people who did, after the corpse was put into the grave, threw in a handful of moulds, saying flaap yie maaht.

After spending a few more tedious weeks here, one of the long-boat-men was taken ill, and the Patroon came and told me I must go with him again to Batavia in his room, which were glad tidings to me; so when we had launched the boat, he mentioned it to the Boatswain, who told him the Captain had received orders from the Commodore not to suffer me off the island during the stay of the English ships that were then in the road. On hearing this, a melancholy gloom seized my spirits, thinking I had lost my liberty for ever: However he insisted that I must go, as he had not hands sufficient to work the boat without me, and at last applied to the Captain for me, from whom he received a positive denial; but by a second application in a short time after, obtained leave, and came to me, saying, the old man has ordered me to take you, and as we shall be there three or four days, you should take some of your clothes with you. I had often conceived a thought in my mind, that this man wished for my enlargement, which I gathered from several intimations he had given, but he always speaking ambiguously, I durst not be so free as to name it, lest I should have been mistaken, and so rivet my own chains. I took nothing with me but my watch-coat, lest I should excite suspicion, and the Captain countermand his order: When we had put off and run out of hail, I thought all was well, and having only 6 leagues to go, we were soon at the place of our destination; and on coming to the quay, the Patroon said, William stay in the boat till I go to the Commodore; and at his return, said to me, now you may go into the town and provide yourself lodgings; I said nay, Christian, I will lay in the boat; to which he answered, you need not, the boys are sufficient for that, therefore go. I thought this was liberty of conscience; so going up into the city, I met an English sailor, to whom I said, what ship, brother? he answered, the *Panther*; I said, do you belong the long-boat? he replied yes; I said, Oh! that's right, I want to go off with you; so walking down together, as we were passing thro' the inner gate into the main-guard, we espyed the Quarter-master in the island-boat; I said, go you on and seem to take no notice of me, and I'll follow at a distance; so he going on, I halted, and then went down to the boat at the quay, and after waiting a while to get opportunity, and conversing with the Quarter-master, I said, I am dry, Christian, I'll go to the booth and get a cup of coffee; he said, do so; I then filed off again as if going amongst the wigwams, and when out of sight, sped me down to the *Panther*'s boat, and to hide appearances (as if I had been boat-keeper) the men began to blast me for absenting myself so long, and then complimented me with a biscuit and some grog. I grew very impatient to be gone, and a little before dark we put off, but at the mouth of the canal, struck so forcibly on the bar, that we shipped a heavy sea, which half filled our boat; on which the Patroon cried out, we are all lost! I said, William, you should not say so, to dishearten the people; so exerting ourselves, we got off into a channel and then into the road; but, being in the wet monsoons, it was very dark, and blowing hard with the wind full in our teeth, (as we term it) some were for putting back, but I endeavoured to dissuade them therefrom, choosing rather to perish, as I apprehended the Dutch might catch me and send me to penguin island, or at least take better care of me. Some were for going on board the *Pococke*, which lay to leeward of us; however we at last came to a grappling in the road, but the boat being deep loaded, and riding hard in a great swell, shipped large seas, and was frequently like to fill, so that some of us were continually at work to bail the water out; and having some bread and arrack, we kept refreshing ourselves, and rode out the storm until morning, when we weighed and turned to windward, till it veering round to the eastward, we laid our course and gained our ship at Kyeper's (or Cooper's) island, where she lay at the wharf about 12 o'clock, when going on the quarter-deck, I acquainted the commanding officer, Lieutenant Garrah, who I was and whence I came, who said to me, you are now safe enough; I said, Sir, I am sensible of it; so calling for the Captain's Clerk and Purser's Steward, ordered each of them to set me down in their respective books, and the Boatswain's Mate to pipe to dinner, and it being Sunday, we had calavanches and pork, in the afternoon we got the guns in, so concluded the day. The Dutch East India Company owe me 60 guilders, or 5 pounds, which I suppose they will never pay.

When we had finished taking in our stores, we left Kyeper's island, and again moored our ship in Batavia road, where we took on board so much arrack, that we had not sufficient room left to slow water enough to serve us on our passage to Madrass. I helped to sling above 100 leagers of it, although it is contrary to the articles of war and the rules of the navy, to take any merchandise on board a king's ship except silver, gold, or diamonds, for the greater security of the owners. Our Captain and two of the Lieutenants were concerned in this business: The death of the former prevented an arrest, but the two latter were seized by Captain Collins of the *Weymouth*, and sent home prisoners; and on their arrival in England, were tried and found guilty of the offence, and were, by the sentence of the court martial, broke and cashiered for the same.

Rear Admiral Cornish, after the conquest of Minilla, had returned to the coast of Coromandel, where he some time after received advice of the Peace, together with his letters of re-call, and so soon as it was convenient, sailed for Europe in the *Norfolk* of 74 guns, accompanied by all the ships under his command, except the *Medway*, *Weymouth*, *Panther*, and *York*, each of 60 guns, and the

Argo of 32 guns, which were necessarily detained in the country to enforce the final adjustment and settleing of some national arrangements with some of the nabobs of Bengal, for which purpose they sailed to Calcutta, except the *Panther*, which was ordered to proceed to Minilla with some Spanish prisoners, and then to Batavia to heave down; but being met by the Monsoons in the China seas, she did not accomplish it, but put back to Batavia, and was hove down at Ondross; and Captain Matthison dying while we were in the road, we put the ship into mourning, and on his corpse going a-shore for interrment, fired minute-guns during the ceremony, which added much to the solemnity. Here, on the 25th of January, 1764, I had the misfortune to get my right leg jamned with the chyme of a cask in the long-boat along side the ship while I was slinging water for the passage to Madrass, which has caused me an infinitude of trouble, and after all, terminated in an amputation of the limb.

We left Batavia the latter end of February, and touching at Prince's island, got wood and water; then putting to sea again, arrived at Madrass on the 4th of April, the other three 60 gun ships still remaining at Calcutta; and four months after, the *Medway* and *Weymouth* returned into the road armed enflute, they and the *York* having landed their lower-deck guns at Fort William. Soon after, Captain Collins appointing Captain Lary to command the *Panther*, she and the *Weymouth* sailed for Trincamale, to wood and water in their way to Europe; and I with 14 others who were not fit to remove, were left behind, and entered in the books of the *Medway*, commanded by John Bladen Tinker, Esq. the *York* being detained at Bengal till Governor Vansitart had settled his affairs there, when taking him on board, she sailed, (leaving the *Argo* still there) and joined us; and as he intended to take the remaining part of his passage in our ship, he very generously and humanely procured and gave to both ships' companies such necessaries as were most needful to guard us against the cold. We sailed in concert with the *York* on the 15th of Feb. 1765, and arrived at the Cape on the 29th of March, and left it again on the 3d of May, shaping our course for St. Helena, where we came to anchor on the 18th. The same day as we were hoisting out the barge, while the ship was going before the wind at the rate of eight or nine knotts, the yard-tackles unhooking, she swang off, and oversetting, filled, with three men in her, one of which ran up the side by the stay-tackle; another went a-stern and caught hold of the life bouy; but the others was drowned. Captain Tinker being the senior officer, ordered Captain Caldwell to sail on the 25th and proceed to Ascension to catch tortoise for both ships' use; and on the 1st of June, we sailed, and joined him there on the 8th, yet we did not come to anchor, but lay to till we had got on board our share of the fish, amounting to 48 tortoises, and the *York* had got up her anchor; then taking our departure, in a few days once more crossed the equator into the northern hemisphere; when, although the *York* was leaky and we were entering the stormy Atlantic, Captain Tinker very ungenerously left her because she sailed heavily; and keeping company with her, lost time, and was likely to have impeded our passage. We arrived at Spithead on the 25th of July, and she at Plymouth on the 5th of August. My leg having been variously better and worse during the passage, occasioned by the variation of air, climate, and provision, was now very bad, so I was sent ashore to the royal hospital at Hazlar, and the ship sent round to Chatham to be paid off. I was placed under the care of the celebrated Surgeon Dodd and Mr Harris, who made a cure of my wound; and being discharged out of the hospital, November 26, I waited on Commissioner Hughes at his office in the dock-yard, to know how I was to get after my ship, who ordered me back till the 12th of December, when he sent a boat for me, which put me on board the *Lion* transport bound to Sheerness; and coming thither, I acquainted the Master Attendant, that Commissioner Hughes had sent me round from Portsmouth; on which he ordered the passage-boat to take me to Chatham, where, on the 2d of Jan. 1766, I received of Commissioner Hanway the wages due to me for the *Panther* and *Medway*. On the 7th, being the first Tuesday in the month, I also received 6 pounds smart-money, from the worshipful Governors of the naval chest, and a pension-ticket for 6 pounds a year, commencing from lady-day 1764, being the first quarter day after the hurt was received, and to appear again in three years.

> How little do the land-men know
>   Of what we sailors feel,
> When seas do mount and winds do blow
>   But we have hearts of steel.

No danger can affright us,
  No enemy shall flout,
We'll make our cannons right us,
  So toss the can about.

Agreeable to my proposal, I shall hereafter give some definition of nautical terms, but before I conclude this part of my work, I must present my readers with a descriptive view of his Majesty's royal navy. Ships and vessels of war are either nominated line of battle-ships, frigates, sloops, cutters, yachts, fire-ships, or bomb-ketches, and are of various constructions and dimensions. A first-rate ship having three gun-decks fore and aft, mounts from 100 to 120 guns, (forty-two pounders) or such as carry a round ball of 42lb weight in her lower tier, twenty-four pounders in her middle tier, twelve pounders on her upper deck, and six pounders on the quarter-deck and fore-castle: Besides these, they and all ships of the line are furnished with caranades (which go on slides) on their poops and swivels for their tops; also small arms of every description, such as muskets, blunderbusses, pistols, cutlasses, half-pikes, &c. likewise hand granades to throw on board of an enemy. A first-rate's complement of men is 850, and if she is a flag-ship, an additional number for the purpose of displaying signals from the different mast heads and yard arms to convey the Admiral's orders. A second-rate carries from 90 to 98 guns, thirty-two pounders below, eighteen's on the middle, nine's above, and six's on the forecastle and quarter-deck; Their number of hands is from 750 to 800. Third-rates are such as carry 64, 70, 74, or 80 pieces of ordnance; an 80 gun ship that is a three decker mounts twenty-four pounders, twelve's, nine's, and six's; but ships of 80 guns that are so constructed as to have but two gun decks fore and aft, have thirty-two pounders below, twenty-four's aloft, and nine's on their quarter-deck, &c. their complement of men is 700, and sometimes they have supernumeraies as before mentioned, 74 and 70 gun ships carry thirty-two pounders, eighteen's, and nine's; a 74 has 600 men, and a 70, 520, when each are full manned. The artillery of a 64 is lighter; she has twenty-four pounders, twelve's, and six's, and 480 men. Fourth-rates carry 50 or 60 guns. A 60 gun ship is also of the line, and mounts twenty-four pounders, twelves, and six's, and has 420 men; and if one of these, in a line of battle, be opposed to a first or

second rate of the enemy, hard is her fate. A 50 gun ship carries the
same weight of metal, and 350 men. These ships are not of the line,
but occasionally made use of as though they were, when the
enemy's number of ships exceed ours; in other cases they are used as
frigates. The fifth-rates mount from 32 to 44 guns; those carrying
40 or 44, are of various constructions; some of them have two decks,
others one proper gun deck only: The former carry eighteen
pounders, nine's, and four's, as before described; the latter mount
twelve pounders on the main-deck and six's on the quarter-deck
and fore-castle. – These last mentioned are by far the best ships;
they carry 250 men each when their complement is complete. A
frigate of 36 guns bears the same metal, and 260 men. One of 32
guns has also twelve and six pounders, with 220 hands. Sixth-rates
have from 20 to 28, and sometimes 30 pieces of cannon, with nine,
and four pounders mostly. A frigate mounting 30 guns, has 210
men; one of 28, has 200; one that is commonly called a 20 gun ship,
has 22 nine pounders and 2 three's on the fore-castle, for bow chase-
guns, and 120 men and boys. Those of less dimension, though some
of them mount 20 guns, bear no rate, but are called sloops and
vessels of war, although from their different moulds and the variety
of their masts and rigging, they might be named ships, snows,
briggs, cutters, doggars, &c. they carry guns and weight of metal
variously, in proportion to their several tonage; from 18, six
pounders, to 16, 14, or 12 ditto, and some 10, others only 8 four
pounders, and men in proportion to their force: In the number of
hands are included boys, as one of these is always necessary to fetch
powder in time of action, to supply the men at each gun. The
artillery made use of in the navy, are such as carry a round ball of 2,
3, 4, 6, 9, 12, 18, 24, 32, or 42 pounds weight, and some caronades
are of caliber for 48, 50, and 56 pound balls: Swivels carry 1, 1½, and
2 pound shot, the various sorts of which used for guns of every size,
are round, grape, double head, canister, &c. these are in common
use; but in privateers and letters-of-marque they frequently use
langridge, star-shot, chain-shot, and sliding-shot; and throw stink-
pots and plum-puddings; they too are sometimes mounted with
cohorns and howitziers. Shells and mortars are of different sizes;
which lead me to say something of bomb-ketches, &c. These vessels
are rigged like doggars, having only a main and mizzen-mast, with
a bowsprit, &c. as a fore-mast would impede their use, which is to

bombard towns or forts, by throwing carcases and shells into them
during a siege; and as the mortar-beds are placed in the hold, they
are not of any use at sea; but besides them, these vessels have a number of carriage-guns to fight their way with, and about 60 hands.
Fire-ships are for the purpose of burning a ship or ships in the
enemy's line, &c. and mount 8 guns, and carry 45 men; they have
several ports on each side, which are made to fall down instead of
hauling up, and are provided with grapplings or hooks at their
lower yard arms; and being well stored with combustibles of various kinds, to which a train is laid ready, if a fleet has the
weather-gage, the Commander makes a signal for a fire-ship to
bear down, and for a line of battle-ship to cover her, i.e. keep
between her and her object; also in the mean time to take out the
men except the Captain and a boat's crew, with one to steer, who
should be a good swimmer: When she has gained a proper distance,
the covering ship shoots a-head, then backs his main top-sail and
lays to, when the man at the helm gives the ship a yaw, and jump-
ing overboard, is taken up by the boat; and the Captain having put
the match to the train as he quitted the ship, she then begins to
burn; and falling along side the enemy, and hooking his rigging,
sets him on fire; and when her port ropes are burnt to let the ports
fall, the fire issues from each of them in a stream; and the covering
ship having taken up the boat, falls again into her station. – If one
of these be taken when her train is laid, the men are mostly hanged
at the yard-arms by the enemy. Yachts are small neat vessels
designed for the use of the royal family and such as are occasionally
attendant on it, and one of them it appropriated to the service of the
Commissioner of each of the principal dock-yards.

It may not be amiss to give my readers some idea how guns that
weight from $5\frac{1}{2}$ to 60 cwt. and upwards, are managable: They are
for that purpose mounted on strong carriages with four trucks or
clog wheels, proportioned to the size and weight of the gun, with a
curve in each side for the trunions to rest in; near which, lower
down on the side, is a ring-bolt and an eye-bolt, and another in the
cross piece, on which the train of the gun rests; and also a ring-bolt
and an eye-bolt in the ship's side near the port, on each side of it; to
the ring-bolt there is seized a strong piece of rope, which is led thro'
that on one side the carriage, then passed through a thimble which
is strapped and seized to the pummilion, then through that on the

other side the carriage, and fastened to that on the other side the port: This we call a breeching; its use is to prevent the gun from running in too far when we have the lee gage, and to help to secure her when she is housed; and for each of the carriages we have a four-fall tackle on either side between the before mentioned eye-bolts, to run her out with when loaded, and partly to secure her when out of action: We have also a tackle hooked to the eye-bolt in the train of the carriage, and to a ring-bolt on the deck, to prevent it running out before the gun is loaded, when on the weather-gage, which we call a relieving-tackle. In the middle of the breech-ring and muzzle-ring, there is a notch to direct us in pointing forward and aft; and at equal distances on each side the said rings, is another notch, to direct in elevating or settling the train, which is performed by the use of an iron crow and a hand-spike; and the position is kept by placing the bed and quoin, which are made of wood for that use. It is always necessary that he who points the gun should have judgment of the ship's motion, to do execution; for if the side be rising, he must take his aim below the water's edge, or he'll fire over the object; if it be lowering, he must level above the gun-wale, or else he will fire into the water: Some attention must also be had to the motion of the object; it is not like fighting ashore.

Before I can proceed to define the line of battle, I must say something about colours, signals, &c. The colours in common use are the jack, ensign, and pendant. Before the union of those kingdoms which now compose Great Britain, the English colours were a white field, with a red cross conjugate and transverse, which we now call the St. George's jack; and the Scotch was a blue field, with a white cross from corner to corner; and at the aforesaid union, the colours of the two nations were so disposed as to form one flag, in which both were blended, so as to preserve a semblance of that agreement, and is therefore called the union-flag. A small flag of this sort is called a jack, and mostly displayed on a staff at the bowsprit end; but as we have three sorts of ensigns in use, I must be particular, because these make the distinction in the divisions of a fleet, &c. They are either a red field, with an union in the upper corner next the staff; a St. George's field, i.e. white with the red cross and the union as above; or a blue field, with the union in the upper and inner corner: It is hoisted on a staff at the tafler or tafrail, and hangs over the stern. The common pendant is composed of three stripes, red, white, and blue, with a red and white cross at the head, being long and narrow; it is kept flying at the main top gallant-mast head of every private ship in commission. Every ship has a great number of plain flags, pendants, &c. of various colours, together with the common colours of every other nation, to display from the different top-mast heads, yard-arms, mizzen peak, &c. as occasion may require; which is sometimes done with and sometimes without the firing of a gun. Every ship has a stern or poop-lanthorn, and those that are of the line have two quarter-lanthorns, and such as are designed for flag-ships have one in their main top; besides which, they have each a number of large lanthorns to fix in the shrouds, or at the mizzen peak, &c. as signals in the night, when sometimes one, two, or more guns are fired, according to appointment; for the common signals are known to every officer in the fleet, as they have books with portraits of ships displaying them variously as occasion may require, and specifying how many guns are to be fired for directing certain acts and manœuvres: False fires too are sometimes used in the night. But as these public signals may be known by an enemy, it is necessary to have some that are of a private nature, the signification of which an enemy cannot acquire: These the commander of a fleet appoints, and his secretary sends a written copy of them to each captain serving under his command respectively.

I now must say something respecting admiralty, or the order of superiority and inferiority of those gentlemen to whom the command of fleets or squadrons is given, when such are appointed on a cruise or an expedition. A Commodore hoists a red broad pendant, with a swallow tail, at the main topgallant-mast head; he is inferior to a Rear Admiral, tho' his pay is the same. The lowest Flag Officer is Rear Admiral of the blue division; next to him is Rear Admiral of the white; and next to that Rear Admiral of the red: These all hoist their respective flags at the mizzen top-mast head, and bring up the rear in the order of sailing. The next is a Vice Admiral of the blue; next to him, Vice Admiral of the white; and then Vice Admiral of the red: These carry their respective flags at the fore-top gallant mast head, and sail in the van when regular order is strictly observed, and they have not a chief command. Next to Vice Admiral of the red, is Admiral of the blue, and then Admiral of the white, which is the highest flag in common use at the main, as the red flag is never hoisted but as a signal, when it is called the bloody flag, signifying that no quarter will be given, and is seldom used but by pirates, though I have known an instance of it's being used by a Rhode-island privateer engaged with a French frigate in the bight of Leogane Hispanola. To supply this defect, the union-flag is occasionally hoisted by a dignified Admiral, such as the first Lord of the Admiralty, or the Lord High Admiral of Great Britain, when he commands a fleet in person: These all carry their respective flags at the main topgallant-mast head, and sail with their proper squadron in the centre of the fleet. As suppose a fleet to consist of 33 sail of the line, forming three divisions, commanded by an Admiral, a Vice Admiral, and a Rear Admiral, each commanding a squadron of 11 ships; the Vice Admiral should sail in the van, and in the night shew lights from his main-top and two quarter-lanthorns, to give direction to the other ships: The Admiral should keep in the centre, and shew a light in his top and each of his three stern-lanthorns; and the third in company, bringing up the rear, should shew a light in his top and poop-lanthorn, to those of his own division that may be a stern of him; though, on the contrary tack, this order must be reversed, and often is in a line of battle.—I have been very particular respecting these things, as I know persons unaccustomed to them form crude ideas, both of them and every such thing as they have not seen; and must further observe, that in a naval engagement, the order is varied by contingent circumstances, such as having the wind, or the lead, or which tack they are on. The commander in chief always gives a plan of his intentions to each subordinate commander, and it is a general rule for the senior Captain of the Vice Admiral's division to lead the van when the line is formed with the starboard tacks on board, and the senior Captain in the rear division to lead where it is formed with the larboard tacks on board, each flag officer being in the centre of his respective squadron. Suppose the afore-mentioned fleet, attended by six sail of frigates, to be standing W. S. W. close hauled, with their larboard tacks on board, (the wind being at south) to descry an enemy's fleet of equal force to leeward, the Commander would then make a signal to form a line of battle a-breast, and so to give chase, edging away until all the ships should have gained their stations; and then bearing down in a body (supposing the enemy to lay to, form a line, and prepare for action) when he shall have gained a proper position so as to have a prospect of engaging with advantage and effect, he then takes in the signal for a line a-breast and displays one for a line of battle a-head; when each ship luffing up to the wind, they fall into a straight line a-head of each other, with their broad-sides directly opposed to those in the enemy's line they are respectively to engage; and as the Admiral's ships are in the centre of their squadron, their signals cannot be seen in time of action, for smoke, each of them have a frigate stationed at a convenient distance a-breast of his beam, to repeat them; so that if he sees a ship in his line overmatched, he displays a signal for the ship nearest a-head to back his mizzen top-sail and drop a-stern, or the ship next a-stern to fill his main top-sail and shoot a-head to relieve her; which signal the frigate (lying in view of the whole fleet) repeats, and keeps flying till it is answered; and if a ship has lost her top-masts, or is otherwise disabled, and thereby in danger of being taken, he makes a signal for one of the other frigates to bear down and take her in tow to convey her out of danger, and afford her assistance, if necessary, till the fate of the day be determined. This brief description may at present suffice, and I will now say something of the rules and customs of the navy.

In order to be a little explicit, I must now observe, that when a fleet or a single ship is so fortunate as to engage and take a prize or prizes, and bring it or them safe into port, if such ship or ships be constructed for vessels of war, they are surveyed by a master builder and other assistants skilled in naval architecture; and if they, on such survey, deem the said ship or vessel useful and fit, they then conjointly with the commissioner of the port yard there, purchase her or them for his Majesty's service, and the purchase-money is always duly and punctually paid in a short time to the captors by certain agents appointed to make such payment; besides which, there is a certain allowance made by government according to the number of artillery mounted on board the captured vessel, if she belonged to government service when taken, and the number of men born on her books, which is called gun-money and head-money; but if the capture be a merchant vessel or privateer, then an agent or agents are chosen by a majority of the captors, and he or they is or are empowered by letter of attorney, to appraise, sell, and dispose of the said capture or captures, by auction or other public sale, and pay the money arising from such sale to the captors respectively, according to the share each man or boy is entitled to by the station or capacity he serves in on board his ship: The proportion of the respective shares is briefly as follows; to a Flag Officer or Officers, one-eighth of the capture; to a Captain or Captains, two-eights; to the Commission-Officers, one-eight; to the Petty-Officers, one-eighth; and the remaining two-eights or one-fourth is divided amongst the foremast-men and such as share with them; and if a Captain has a roving commission or act independent of the orders of an Admiral, he is in that case entitled to three-eighths of the capture. An agent is allowed six months to dispose of the ship and cargo of a prize, before he is obliged to make any payment of money to the captors, and to give public notice some time previous to each payment he proposes to make, whether of the whole or part of such capture; and if after the last advertisement, any share or dividend remain unclaimed for the space of three years, it is forfeited and becomes comes payable towards the maintenance of Greenwich hospital.

With respect to wages, I shall only say, that an Admiral has 3l. 10s. per day; a Vice Admiral, 2l. 10s, a Rear Admiral, 1l. 15s. a Commodore, the same; a Captain of a first-rate, 23s. per day, or 39l. 4s. per month, consisting of 28 days; of a second-rate, 33l. 12s. of a third-rate, 28l. of a fourth-rate, 22l. 8s. of a fifth-rate, 16l. 16s. of a sixth-rate, 11l. 4s. and a Master Commander, the same; Lieutenants, 5s. per day; and Masters and other officers of inferior rank have monthly pay in proportion to the rate of the ships to which they respectively belong; but the pay of a Quarter-gunner is only 1l. 5s. (one of which is allowed to every 4 guns) that of an able seaman, 1l. 4s. and that of an ordinary seaman or landman, 19s. per month, out of which is reserved 6d. for Greenwich hospital, 4d. for the Chaplain, 2d. for the Doctor, and 6d. for the Purser for the supply of bowls, platters, cans, spoons, candles, and pudding-bags; and if a man miss a muster when in port, a cheque is put against his name; if he miss two musters, a second cheque; and the third time, an R is affixed by the clerk of the cheque, when all his pay and arrears of pay are deemed forfeited and made due to the chest at Chatham.

When a wound is received or a hurt sustained on board a ship, or on shore in the service of such ship, it is the Surgeon's duty (previous to the wounded or hurt seaman's leaving the ship to go to any hospital or on board of any hospital-ship) to fill up or make out a smart-ticket for him, specifying such wound or hurt, and how and on what act of duty it was received, signed by the Captain, first Lieutenant, Master, Surgeon, Purser, Boatswain, Gunner, and Carpenter (bearing an emblem of a man standing on a chest on one leg, and having lost an arm on the opposite side) which the patient, when cured and permitted to go, must present to the governors of the naval chest at Chatham, who have a discretionary power to award a sum of money, as smart, and dismiss the man if they deem it too trivial for a pension; and also what pension they suppose adequate to the hurt, where it is a casual one; but where an eye or a limb is lost, they have slated rules to go by, although in casualities they can either augment, diminish, or strike off the list, after the expiration of the first granted pension-ticket, which is sometimes at the end of a year, but generally of three years, and where a limb is lost, of five years; for which reason, they have appointed a review at the chest, to commence on the first Tuesday in every month, except on Christmas Day; when and where such of the pensioners, whose tickets are expiring or have expired, are required to attend, give in their old tickets, and receive new ones according to the governors' discretion; and if any one has lost his ticket, he must draw up and present a petition for a new one, which will be granted. When I was first put upon the list, the rules were, to allow smart-money equal to a whole year's pension, and the pension to commence from the first quarter day after the hurt was sustained, and to be continued to those who obtained cooks' warrants; but during the American war, when every plan of national œconomy was deemed necessary, it was taken off, and only half a year's pension for smart allowed, and every one obliged to appear at the end of one year after his ticket was out, although prior to that period we were connived at if we stayed two years over our time, as the governors would pay one year after the expiration of the ticket, and we might go at the end of another and our certificate or letter of life only needed to be signed by the minister and church-warden of the parish where we respectively resided; but afterwards (I suppose on the discovery of some fraudulent practices) it was required, that each should make attestation before a justice of the peace or a chief magistrate, and sign it also himself, that such signature might be compared with that in the chest power; and if there was but one churchwarden, for him to sign himself sole and only churchwarden, and that each pensioner must appear to review about the time his ticket expires, on pain of suspension until he does appear. If any are struck off the list, it is generally with half a year's pension advance. The old rules are in part again adopted, I believe. At one of these reviews, what a shocking spectacle presents itself to the eyes of the spectator! Here you may behold perhaps 500 mutilated creatures of different ages and appearances, some clean and decently appareled; some dirty and almost naked, so that all the cloaths on their backs would scarcely make a kitchen-girl a mop; some with meager and emaciated looks, appear as if they never had a good meal of meat, while here and there one indeed retain some faint vestiges of their former likeness; some have lost an eye, and others both; some have a hand, some an arm off; some, both near the wrists, some, both close to the shoulders; others, one at the wrist and the other above the elbow; some are swinging on a pair of crutches; some with one wooden leg below the knee; another above the knee; some with one leg off below the knee and the other above; some with a hand off and an eye out; another with an eye out and his face perforated with grains of battle-powder, which leave as lasting an impression as though they were injected by an Italian artist; some with their limbs contracted; others have lost part of a hand or part of a foot; some have a stiff knee from a fracture of the petella bone; some have lost the tendons, and others, flesh, from their arm-pits; while another has lost a piece from the back of his neck; another has had his scull fractured and trepanned, and a silver plate substituted in the room of what was taken out; some with their noses shot off; others with a piece torn from the cheek; another with his jaw bone or chin shot off, &c. &c. &c. A gentleman once observed to me, he wondered why all or most of the pensioners did not reside near the chest, that they might attend without so much inconvenience! His notion was plausible and well meant; but were such a measure adopted, the cities of London and Westminster, and the whole counties of Kent, Essex, Middlesex, Surry, Berks, and Sussex, would be inhabited with little else than a motley company of halt, maimed, blinkards, and cripples: Who then would carry on the manufactures and drive the Lord Mayor's coach?

As it is my wish to promote, and not depress, his Majesty's service, I must beg of my readers to have a little patience while I observe, that all the poor wretches before mentioned are not abandoned or obliged to take only a small pension, as there is another asylum provided for them who are most disabled by loss of limbs or other extreme hurts sustained in the service, and also those who have worn out their best days and spent their strength Britannia's weal to save; – I mean the Royal Hospital at Greenwich, which magnificent building is not to be equaled in the world, and its endowment is equal to its magnificence; its situation is eligible, close by the fine river Thames, where ships pass and repass; the air is salubrious, the park delightful, the chapel elegant, the clothing for the pensioners comfortable, and the provision wholesome and plentiful; all which conspire to render life, loaded with infirmities, tolerable if not happy in its decline, 'when safe moor'd in Greenwich tier.' Some almost worn out Admiral is, in succession, governor of this grand asylum; besides which, there is another Flag Officer sub-governor. The men have little more to do than behave themselves well; and when they are disorderly, they are sometimes made to wear a yellow coat with red sleeves, or some other badge of disgrace, and are appointed to sweep the square, &c. If any obtain leave of absence, the sub-governor has his allowance during that period. They have also 1s. per week for tobacco; and many have an out-pension from the hospital for long servitude, which is about 7l. a year. Every man and boy in British sea-pay contribute 6d. per month out of that pay towards the maintenance of this grand naval hospital: Though none can claim or ought to have admittance into it but such as have served in the royal navy, yet some time ago, many gentlemen, through interest, gained admittance for their worn-out domestics who had never been at sea in their lives, consequently these had no right, if a merchant's man who pays to its, support has none or is allowed none; but these abuses are now reformed.

As I purpose to expose to view a striking figure of the wooden world, I must present to my readers some account of the order, discipline, allowance, &c. and shall begin with discipline. As to small crimes or misdemeanors committed on board merchant ships, they are recognisable before a common court of judicatory, or the magistracy of the port or place the ship or vessel may belong to, be at, or put into; but matters of a higher nature or greater degree of criminalty, such as mutiny, murder, or piracy, are to be brought to trial before a court of admiralty, which is mostly held at the Old Bailey or Doctors' Commons for London, and sometimes for other ports, if the nature and degree of the offence require it; but on board any of his Majesty's ships and vessels of war, small crimes and misdemeanors may be forgiven or punished by the Captain or Master Commander, who can, agreeable to the articles of war, enforce order or discipline, by various modes or means. Boys are sometimes stripped and seized by the left hand to a hoop, when three or four have been guilty of the same offence, and a nittle given into each of their right hands and made to run round and each flog the boy next before him, so that the harder one is flogged the harder he flogs another: Sometimes they have their breeches or trowsers put down, and are then seized fast to the train of a gun, and punished on their breech by the infliction of an half dozen or a dozen with a cat-of-ninetails; and in certain cases, are obliged to reward the Boatswain's Mate, who inflicts the punishment, with their day's allowance of wine or grog, if at that time they are on either of those allowances. If a man be guilty of notorious lying, he is, according to the rules and orders of the Royal Navy, to be hoisted up to the main-stay by one of the fore braces, with a broom and shovel affixed to his back, and there to hang for the space of half an hour, the people crying all the while, a liar! a liar! and then it is made his duty to clean the seats in the head, which are for the purpose of easing nature, and so he obtains the appellation of liar of the head. And if any are guilty of much profane swearing, the Officers are to forfeit one day's pay for every such offence, but the men are to wear a cangue or wooden collar during the Commanding Officer's pleasure; which collar is composed of two pieces of plank about three inches thick, with a curve to encompass the neck and fasten round it with a lock, and its gravity is increased by four, nine, or twelve pound shots placed' in curves made in a quadrangular form, and fastened in with bits of iron hooping nailed over them; but this is used with partiality:– On board the *Blandford*, Captain Cummings ordered, that the party, attended by the Master at Arms, should walk the lee side of the quarter-deck until he should hear another swear; so that they would often stagger with design, and tread on the toes of some of the after-guard or main-top men, who perhaps' would say, d–n your eyes, why don't you keep your feet to yourselves? what do you tread on me for? when the prisoner would cry out, Sir, such a man swears! when the collar was immediately taken off him and fixed on the other; till at length the Captain was obliged to reform the abuse, by ordering the offender to wear it for a limitted time. Sometimes an exceeding noisy fellow is gagged with a pump-bolt in his mouth confined behind the neck with a piece of spunyarn, and placed in the weather-mizzen shrouds with his face to windward for an hour, or sometimes two hours. A disorderly person they will scrub with a broom in a tub full of water, to make him keep cleanly. The Captain can also cause a thief to run the gantlet; and may, if he pleases, order him to be towed ashore at the boat's stern, with a rope about his neck, and turned adrift: The manner of inflicting this punishment is this; the men have each two rope-yarns given them, of which they make nittles, and cast a half-hitch on the end, then arrange themselves along the dock in two rows at a convenient distance, when the offender being stripped, is caused to pass between them, and each man is obliged to strike him with the nittle as he passes along; and in some cases they are made to ascend and descend the quarter deck and forecastle ladders, at each of which á Boatswain's Mate is placed with a cat, who flogs them during that time, which is very severe: Sometimes the Master at Arms or ship's Corporal walks before them with the point of a naked cutlass at their breasts, to retard their progress. I have seen both these done; the first, on board the *Vengeance*, to two men who had robbed one of our men whose name was Daniel Clegg, while ashore on leave at Plymouth, by capcising him end for end at a public-house, and shaking his money out of his pocket and paying their own reckoning with it. The second, on board the *Winchester*, to one out of three men who had ravished and robbed a girl of the town, whom they met with at No-place, as it is called, about half way between Plymouth and Plymouth dock: She not knowing them, came on board with her complaint, and all hands being called, we were ordered to pass over the quarter-deck, till at length she challenged one whose name was William Edwards, who had been the ringleader and principal actor in the mischief, and he impeached the other two, who not being so guilty as himself, were allowed to run, while he was restrained therefrom by the Corporal's cutlass; and was, after receiving severe punishment, sent ashore and drifted. The Dutch inflict it with slit ratans, but don't strip the offender to the skin, yet if they find them naked they do not allow them to put on their clothes. I saw one run the gantlet naked, in the

East Indies, between two very long ranks, the Commander in Chief
sitting in an easy chair to see it: The poor wretch, who had been
Boatswain of one of their Indiamen, would sometimes essay to cast
himself prostrate at his feet, and when in that attitude, the old gentleman would shew his masticators, and with a stern countenance
and uplifted cane, vociferate blackfom vat doon yic heer quamha?
on which he set off and ran again. But in our navy, when a man is
brought to the gangway to be flogged, the Captain cannot exceed a
dozen lashes on the bare back for one offence, without a court martial, which must not consist of less than five Captains, or at least
four Captains and the first Lieutenant of a flag-ship; and if it is to
try an Officer, it must consist of more members and of higher
degree in proportion to the rank and station of such Officer or
Officers as is or are to be tried by such court martial respectively;
the issue of such martial investigation is sometimes a bare acquittal
of the party, and sometimes an honourable acquittal, when it
appears to the court that the prosecution is malicious and the alle-
gations in the charge false and ill founded; but on the other hand, if
the charge or charges be substantiated against a Foremast-man, he
is perhaps sentenced to be flogged from ship to ship, and to receive
a certain number of lashes along side each, and his bleeding back
only covered with a blanket or great coat while going from one to
the other, at the distance of a mile or mile and half, or more, in
which execution of their sentence, they receive 300, 400, 500, 600, or
700 lashes, according to the nature and degree of the offence, or the
determination of the court. Sometimes they are sentenced to be
made jewel-blocks of, i.e. suspended by a rope round their necks at
the fore yard-arm till they are dead, to which exalted station they
are advanced from the cat-head in the smoke of a gun fired on the
occasion, and under the display of a yellow flag at the mast head: If
it be a Warrant-Officer, he is hung at the starboard main-yard arm;
if a Petty-Officer, at the larboard main-yard arm; and such a degree
of honour may be also observed between an able and an ordinary
seaman or landman, Masters, Lieutenants, Commanders, Captains,
and Commodores; and every order of Flag Officers are responsible
to a court martial, and are, by a sentence of such court, sometimes
suspended, sometimes broke, at other times broke and cashiered of
their wages, and sometimes punished with death; the said sentence
being grounded on a breach of some particular article or articles of

war, and then death inflicted by a file of marines discharging their loaded pieces at the breast of the unhappy object, who receives it on his knees. As I went in the barge, it gave me an opportunity of attending at many courts martial, of which our Captain was a member. I shall mention two or three instances. At one of these courts held in Portsmouth harbour, on board the *Newark* of 80 guns, two prisoners were tried who belonged to the *Woolwich* of 40 guns, both for desertion, and one who was a Captain's servant, for purloining some property from his master; the issue of which trial closed in a sentence, that one should receive 600 and the other 700 lashes from ship to ship along side such of his Majesty's ships and vessels of war as were then at Spithead and in the harbour or in dock. The servant, on hearing his sentence pronounced by the judge advocate, addressed himself to the court, and in the most humble and pathetic manner requested he might be hanged! Being asked his reason for such request, he replied, I cannot endure the punishment. On which Sir William Burnaby answered with a degree of severity in his looks, the sentence contains no more than what the court has thought fit to impose, and dead or alive it must be carried into execution. The punishment was to be inflicted at three times on three fortnight days; we attended them through the process of the first day, when one of our marines on guard in the bow of the boat fell asleep and lost the bayonet off the muzzle of his piece, and narrowly escaped getting a dozen for his offence: We sailed before another fortnight day. At another of these courts, three young men were tried and sentenced to receive 300 each, from ship to ship, for having gone from the post of duty assigned them: They belonging to the *St George*, and going in the barge, had made a practice of carrying liquor off and selling it among the ship's company at an exorbitant price; and to punish them for their offence, Captain Gayton lent them for a channel-cruise on board the *Baslick* bomb-vessel, and they disliking their new ship, which after the accomplishment of her cruise was ordered into dock at Portsmouth, left her and went over land to Deal; and the *St George* being then stationed in the Downs, they were again received on board her, the Captain being inclined to excuse the impropriety of their conduct; but when the Master and Commander of the *Baslick* came to know of them being there, he requested of the Lords of the Admiralty that they might be tried by a court martial; and

although Captain Gayton used his interest in their behalf, he could
not prevail to have their crime dispensed with, or their punishment remitted or in the least mitigated, although they respectively
bore good characters. At another of these courts held on board the
Newark, the Captain, Lieutenant, and Master of the *Mermaid* were
tried for the loss of the said ship on the Beheima bank, when the
two former were acquitted with honour, they having done their
duty in using their utmost endeavours to save her, but the latter
was convicted of having neglected so to do, and also quitting her in
distress; likewise of having encouraged part of the crew to desert
her while there yet remained a probability of getting her off; for
which offences he was broke and ordered to do his duty before the
mast. At another court martial, a Lieutenant of a cutter was tried
and broke for contempt of his office and of his superior; the occasion was this – the *Launceston* and us being on a cruise in the
channel, we brought the cutter to, off Lime-reigus, when the
Captain of the *Launceston*, as Commodore (he being the senior
officer) ordered the cutter's boat to be got out and the Commander
to come on board his ship; which being complied with, and the
Lieutenant being without his uniform and neither sword nor
cockade, was asked, who commands that cutter? he answered, I
do, Sir, instead of a better. The Captain then asking him why he
came on duty without those badges of his office, he like a
Wappineer tar replied, I am as good a man without them as with
them. For which contumacious answer the Captain laid him under
an arrest, and sent one of his own Lieutenants to succeed him in
his command, and kept him prisoner on board his ship till he
arrived in port to bring him to trial.

Provisions and allowance-money. – Every man and boy borne
on the books of any of his Majesty's ships, are allowed as follows,
viz. a pound of biscuit-bread and a gallon of beer per day; on
Tuesday and Saturday 2lb. of beef, or else 1lb. of beef and 1lb. of
flour with plums for a pudding; (frequently four or six mess
together, when for every two, 4lb. of meat or pudding is allowed)
on Thursdays and Sundays, every two has a 3lb. piece of pork and
each a pint of pease to boil into soup; the other three days are called
banian days, in allusion to a people in Asia who always abstain
from the use of animal food, and are known by the name of
Banians; on each of these days we have 2 oz. of butter and $\frac{1}{4}$ lb. of

Cheshire cheese; and on Wednesdays, $\frac{1}{2}$ a pint of gort or ground oat-meal boiled into burgoo for breakfast, and a pint of pease to make soup for dinner; on Monday we have no pease, but have our burgoo for dinner. When ships are abroad they cannot get beer, but have an allowance of that sort of liquor which the country produces in lieu thereof, viz. if they are on a long cruise in the home seas and their beer is expended, they have $\frac{1}{2}$ a pint of brandy and $1\frac{1}{2}$ pints of water mixed into grog; if they be in the West Indies, they have an equal quantity of rum-grog; in the East Indies, of arrack-grog; but in the Mediterranean seas or at the Cape of Good Hope, the daily allowance is a pint of white wine mixed with another of water, and served out at twice, either at breakfast and dinner or dinner and 4 o'clock in the afternoon. They are now allowed a quantity of molasses to eat with their burgoo to prevent the use of salt beef fat, which generated the scurvy. But as every species of provision is liable to either waste or leakage, their several weights and measures made use of are no more than seven-eights, to indemnify the Purser against loss, so that the gallon is only 7 pints and the pound 14 ounces. The Steward makes a fresh mess-book every month, so that the men can change their mess-mates as often as they please; and when he serves their beef or pork, he calls forward one day and backward the next, to give them an equal chance of time to eat it. As to the manner of serving, it is this – they give a man liberty to choose a piece for his mess, and then hoodwink him, and when the Steward calls a mess, he touches a piece, and the Cook gives it to the man it is for, and he touches again. Some years ago they used to put the meat into a tub and cover it with a cloth and each prick for his lot with the tormentors, but this often tore it to pieces. Each mess has a mark for its pudding-bag, which is put to when it goes to the Cook. If any species of provision is deemed unwholesome and unfit to be used, it is to be surveyed by at least three Masters in the navy, and if it be found so, they condemn it to be started and thrown overboard. And if at any time we are detained at sea beyond what we expected, so that we apprehend a likelihood of scarcity, it becomes necessary to go on short allowance, and generally three men subsist on what two should have; and in extreme cases, on still less: When it is partial and only of one or two articles, we are paid in kind as soon as a supply is obtained, but if it be a general scarcity we are allowed 5s. a month short allowance-money, so soon as we

come where there is an Agent-victualler. I never received more of
this kind of arrearage than 10s. on my return from the West Indies
in the *Blandford*, which was paid me by the Agent-victualler at
Plymouth. Soldiers deemed passengers, and prisoners of war, while
they remain on board are kept on shorto.

I shall now say a little about equipage and ceremonies. When an
Officer is coming on board or going out of a ship, entering-ropes
knotted with diamond knots and covered with red baize are put
down by the gangway sleps, and the side is manned with a number
of hands according to the superiority or inferiority of the Officer
ascending or descending it, viz, for a Flag-Officer or Captain, six;
for a Lieutenant or Master, four; and for a Warrant-Officer or
Petty-Officer, two: And sometimes on a Commander in Chief or
other person of high rank coming on board, a guard is mounted
and manœuvre as he ascends the gangway; if it be in the night, each
of the men hold a lanthorn in their hands to light him up, in order
to know who is coming as well as his rank in office; the Quarter-
master of the watch hails the boat while at a convenient distance,
and asks if she is coming on board? when if she is not, the
Cockswain answers, no; but if she be, and has the Captain in, he
pronounces the ship's name to which such Captain belongs; if it is a
Commission-Officer, he says aye, aye! and if one of inferior order,
no, no! When a lady is coming on board, she is fixed in an elegant
chair neatly slung with red rope and run up with a whip, i.e. a rope
reeved through a tail-block fastened to the main yard for that purpose, then hauled in and landed on the gangway, where she is
received by the Commanding-Officer and led aft. Sometimes we
have an accommodation-ladder over the side in fine weather while
in harbour, which is of very easy ascent. The Boatswain and his
mates have each a silver pipe or call which they fix to the button-
hole of their coat or jacket with a ribbon, with which they call the
watch or all-hands, and direct almost every act of duty that is performed in the ship, such as hoisting or lowering of casks, bales, &c.
hoisting boats in or out, swaying up yards and top-masts, veering
away cable, heaving up anchors, palling the capstan, setting sails,
stoppering or belaying ropes, manning the side, calling the sweep-
ers and scavenger, piping to breakfast or dinner, &c. in short almost
every thing is conducted by the vibration of the call as much as soldiers are directed through their several evolutions by beat of drum,

which noisy instrument is not much used in the navy, except when a fleet is at mooring and under the command of one or more Admirals, where it is usual for the drums to beat about day-break and continue until we can see a grey goose a mile, when the flag-ship fires a gun. At sun-rise every ship in the fleet hoists her colours, viz. her ensign and jack, unless it blows hard, and the yards and top-masts are struck, in which case the colours are not hoisted but when some vessel is coming in or passing; and at sun-set they are again struck or hauled down; at half past 7 o'clock the drums begin to beat and continue till 8, when the ship on board of which the Commander in Chief hoists his flag, fires a gun, which is answered by the discharge of a volley of small arms from those of every subordinate Flag-Officer. On certain rejoicing days, such as his Majesty's birth-day, &c. each ship that composes part of the fleet fires a royal salute of 21 guns, in succession, one every minute, taking the motion from the Admiral, who fires first precisely at 1 o'Clock; this we term a Spithead fight, or a battle without bloodshed. The French use the call in their boats, by which the Cockswains of barges and pinnaces, and the Patroons of launches and long-boats direct the men in their several motions when putting off or coming along side a ship or wharf laying on a beach, &c. It is a common custom in the sea-service, on making or descrying any cape or headland of consequence, to make all the men and boys in the vessel who have not before seen it, pay a bottle of liquor and a pound of sugar to mix into bumbo or toddy for themselves and the rest of the crew; and on crossing the equator, they pay the same, which payment frees them of every promontory situate in the northern hemisphere, but not of those beyond the line; and if any one refuse to comply with this usage, he is to be ducked after the following manner, viz. a tail-block is fixed out at the arm of the main yard, through which a rope is reeved, and a sling made near the end of it by a running bowline knott, in which the man is placed with a toggle fixed over his head to prevent his being run up too high; then the fall is led through a block at the quarter of the yard, and another fastened to a ring-bolt on the deck, and so fore and aft; and he is gently run up and eased off with a guy, then let run into the water and presently hoisted up again; suffered to take his breath, and let go down a second time; and after the third dip, they hoist him high enough and then haul him in with the guy and release him; but this ceremony is never observed on board any ship or vessel belonging to his Majesty's royal navy. The Dutch have a method of punishing some particular crimes by keel-hauling, viz. they take a sufficient length of rope and pass one end of it round the cut-water and let it fall under the bottom, then reeve the ends at both the yard-arms as before mentioned, and over-hauling the bight, fix the man in the middle of it, with a deep sea-lead fastened to his heels for the purpose of sinking him clear of the ship's keel: They then run him up and let go, and allowing sufficient time for the lead to sink him deep enough, he is run up on the other side, permitted to breathe a little, and sent a second time under the bottom; and when he has dived three times, he is hauled in, some refreshment given him, and then put to his hammock. This barbarous punishment is rarely inflicted but for aggravated offences perpetrated by extraordinary bad characters, and never used in our service, although it must be acknowledged we have often recourse to severity.

A ship's company is generally divided into equal parts, which are thus denominated – The starboard watch and larboard watch; of the former, the Master of a merchant ship takes the immediate charge, and the Mate of the latter; but if the vessel be large enough to have a Second Mate, he then takes the Captain's charge and lets him sleep all night. The duration of a watch at sea is four hours, beginning at 8 o'clock at night, which is called the first watch; from 12 to 4, the middle watch; from 4 to 8, the morning watch; from 8 to 12, the forenoon watch; from 12 to 4, the afternoon watch; and that from 4 to 8 is divided into two, called dog watches; the design of which is to prevent one watch having two night watches every twenty-four hours. A trick at the helm is two hours, at the lead half an hour, and at the mast head the same. In East Indiamen where they have six or more Mates and four Midshipmen, they are divided in proportion as well as the men. And in his Majesty's ships and vessels of war, the Lieutenants (who take charge of watches) and the inferior Officers are equally divided; but the Captain, Master, Boatswain, and other Warrant-Officers sleep all night; and there are several who are excused from watching, to occupy their trades, such as the armourer, butcher, barber, &c. who are called idlers, and are occasionally called up to assist the watch when it is not necessary to call all hands; these are in charge of the Master at

Arms and ship's Corporal to turn up when they are called, which in squally weather is frequently three or four times in a watch. These are the common rules, but on board of ships navigating in high latitudes, either for discovery or to fish for whales, &c. they make three watches, to prevent too great an exposure of the men to the intense cold, and avoid the bad effects of it, as they approach either of the poles, and in that case they term them the starboard, larboard, and middle watch. When an anchor-watch is kept, it generally consists of only a Petty-Officer and a few men to keep a look out, and in blowing weather to sland by the sheat-anchor to cut it away if necessary. The Officers correct their time-keepers by the sun when he is in the meridian, and we then ring the bell and turn the four-hour and half-hour glasses and hang them both up, and when the small one is out, we strike one on the bell; when it is out again, two; and so on to seven; and when the large one is out, we ring the bell, call and relieve the watch; but at 4 in the afternoon, only the little glass is turned, and that not for the last half hour; so when it is 8 o'clock by the pocket watches, the bell is rung and both glasses turned for the first watch.

As it may probably happen that this narration may fall into the hands of some young men whose genius and inclination may lead them to think of ploughing the fluid element and exploring the different parts of the globe; for their information I shall just mention some of the rules of entering on such service; and first, if a poor boy be so inclined, either he, for himself, or his friends or relations for him, must bind him apprentice to an owner or master of a ship or vessel for such a time and on such other conditions as parties can agree. Indeed some Captains belonging to the ports of London, Bristol, and Liverpool, will often take sprightly lads on monthly pay at their first going to sea, and if such prove diligent and obliging, they often get to be good seamen; nevertheless those who serve an apprenticeship are in general most esteemed; and some lads who have good parts, and are willing to learn navigation, are frequently put in by their masters as Second Mates, Boatswains, &c. a year or two before they are out of their times, particularly so in vessels employed in the coal-trade. But young gentlemen who have learned the theoretical part of navigation in a good school, and have opulent parents who wish them to be taken into better births or posts of preferment, without submitting to an apprenticeship, or

the drudgery of a boy serving before the mast, if such wish to be in
the service of the honourable united East India company, their ini-
tiation into that employ is in the capacity of a guinea-pig, as they
term it. Their parents or guardians give a premium with them to
the owners or the ship's husband (for the company have no ships of
their own except their men of war and grabbs, with a few packets)
and if such premium so given be about 50 guineas, the boy is put to
mess in the steerage with the third, fourth, and inferior Mates; and
such youths are sometimes put to assist them and the Midshipmen
in their respective duties; but where a premium of 100 guineas or
more is given, the young gentleman messes in the coach or great
cabin with the Captain, Super-cargo, Chief and Second Mates, and
Purser: Such are treated entirely as gentlemen; and so acquiring the
art of seamanship, together with the practical part of navigation,
are often made Mates of the lower order; from thence they may rise
either by their own merit or the interest of friends to be fifth,
fourth, third, second, or Chief Mates, and from thence to be
Captains, whose pay is 30l. per month, and that of a Chief Mate 20l.
But in the Royal Navy they must first go as Midshipmen, in which
station they serve about three years, and then are sometimes made
Masters' Mates, and from thence rise to be Masters or Lieutenants,
though frequently they act as Cadets or Acting Lieutenants for a
while, and then are mostly Supernumeraries on board large ships,
and called seventh or eighth Lieutenants, yet the ship has but six
allowed: From such a station they may rise to be Master
Commander, Post Captain, Captain, Commodore, Rear Admiral,
Vice Admiral, and then Admiral of any of the several divisions of
blue, white, or red, and at last come to be Admiral of England or
Commander in Chief of his Majesty's naval forces; but when this
exalted station is aimed at, alas, how many sail round Cape
Disappointment!!!

I would just observe, that his Majesty's service is, in many
respects, preferable to any other; first, as when a ship in the merchants' service is cast away, the men and officers lose their pay,
except they can save as much of the cargo as will pay them; and if
she is taken by an enemy, their property, pay, and liberty are lost
together, until they recover the latter: But if a king's ship is lost, the
men may thereby lose their little property on board her, yet their
pay goes on if they do not absent themselves from the service; and if

a ship of war be taken, the pay is continued all the time they remain prisoners of war in an enemy's country, and they are better provided for in cases of debility by misfortune or old age. And secondly, the provision is better in kind and more plentiful, for in many foreign traders the allowance is very small, and even in those employed for the East India company, the allowance is only 5lb. of bread a week, and on Tuesdays and Saturdays a 7lb. piece of beef for 5 men (that being the number of every mess) and a 5lb. piece of pork with each a pint of pease or calavanches for soup on Sundays and Thursdays; and on each of the three banian days a portion of stock fish with a proportionate quantity of oil, vinegar, and mustard, to qualify it; and as to beverage, when their beer is expended they go on an allowance of two quarts of water per day, with a pint of punch on Sundays, and every day a dram while they are passing through the Ethiopic sea and Indian ocean; also a quantity of boiled wheat or congee for breakfast for about three weeks while they are going round the Cape. I have been thus particular that each may know what treatment to expect in whatever service he means to engage himself; and would further notice, that if a lad is bound apprentice to the sea and either enters himself or be pressed into his Majesty's sea-service, there is a law which entitles the Master or his heirs, administrators, or assigns, to the wages of such apprentice, for all the time he had to serve such his Master at the time of his entry on board any of his Majesty's ships, to the expiration of his indenture, unless such apprentice was 18 years old when bound by such indenture of apprenticeship. For example – when I was paid the *Blandford*'s wages on board the *Vengeance* in May, 1759, my master having searched the books at the admiralty office to know what ship I belonged to, had, previous to the time of payment, sent my indenture down to Commissioner Rogers at Plymouth, who, on calling me into the cabin, said, are not you 'prentice to Charles Wood? I said, Sir, I was 'prentice to him. He replied, here is your indenture, your master must have your wages. I expostulated with him, but to no purpose, thinking it very hard for him to have the money I had wrought and fought for, venturing life and limbs, as he could not protect me in his service; in particular, I insisted he had no right to it, as I was 18 years old when bound, and consequently entitled to my own pay, by virtue of an abstract of the act of parliament then hanging up under the half-deck of the ship, which abstract every ship in the navy has in her possession. He said that act was enacted since your indenture was drawn, and so cannot reach your case; therefore I was forced to take 19l. 1s. in lieu of 45l. 13s. 6d. which was due to me. Confidence and ignorance betrayed me into this, for I thought my master a gentleman of too much honour to do so mean an action, otherwise I should have used some precaution to prevent it; and Captain Nightingale said if he had been acquainted with it beforehand, he would have set me and Luke Harris (another apprentice) down, run, by which our pay would have been forfeited to the use of the chest at Chatham; and on the returning of our respective indentures to the places whence they came, he would have taken off the R from the ship's book and sent us ashore to receive our money at the recall-office. So I close this part of my performance.

Introduction to Geography

Having closed the first part of my undertaking, I must now proceed to lay before my readers a brief description of those places I have had the opportunity of visiting in the course of my voyages; but in order to be more clearly understood by such of them as have neither travelled nor had the benefit of a liberal education, it may be necessary to lay before them a plain and easy Introduction to Geography, or a short compendium of that useful science.

I know from my own experience that young people often form very weak ideas about the magnitude and motion of the earth, conceiving it impossible for such a vast body to go round the sun, and as impossible for any one to go round it. I confess I was at a loss to conceive how any person could circumnavigate the globe, as I then imagined it to be a flat surface, and that they must be impeded by land or fields of ice, which would render a voyage round the world utterly impracticable; and was, from that ignorance, almost ready to ridicule those who talked about it, although performed by gentlemen of such well-known high characters as Sir Francis Drake, Lord Anson, &c.

I shall begin with a brief description of the solar or Copernican system, which is as follows; the sun, which is an immense body of fire, is the centre of, and gives light and heat to all and each of the seven opaque or dark bodies called planets, which revolve round him in their several orbits, each of which are in the form of an ellipsis, though of very different extent. Mercury, being the smallest and innermost of all the primary planets, makes his revolution round his centre in 2 months and 28 days. Venus is somewhat higher in the system, and performs her revolution round the sun in 7 months and 15 days, and is alternately our morning and evening star: These two are called inferior planets, because they are of less magnitude and their orbs of less compass than the earth's. Terrestria or the earth is next Venus, and describes her ellipsis in 1 year (of which I shall treat more at large hereafter) but she being at a much greater distance from the sun, cannot receive either light or heat in a degree proportionate to the former, and consequently her motion must be

slower: She is constantly attended by the moon, as a secondary
planet, which receives its light and heat from the sun, and reflects it
upon the earth, and this in some measure compensates for the sun's
absence during the winter seasons in the north and south parts of
the world or globe. The other four planets are called superior, from
their greater magnitude and the extent of their orbs, as each of
them include that of the earth. Mars is next to the earth, though
much higher in the solar system, and takes a larger circuit, revolving round the sun in 1 year, 10 months, and 22 days; and from his
fiery aspect, has been called the god of war. Jupiter, which is the
largest of all the planets, performs his revolution round the sun in
about 11 years, 10 months, and 27 days: There are four satellites or
moons moving round him, which, as secondary planets, receive
their light and heat from the source, and reflect it on their primary
planet, as our moon does upon this earth. Observe a Jupiternian
year is almost twelve of our years. Jupiter is also sometimes a morning and evening star. Saturn revolves round the sun in about $29\frac{1}{2}$
years: He has five moons which revolve round him in different
periods of time, and is surrounded with a prodigious ring, which
some suppose to be an atmosphere; and it is natural to imagine that
each of these bodies have an atmosphere, and are habitable systems
or worlds, as they are found subject to the same laws of nature as
this in which we live; but if so, the inhabitants must have constitutions very different from ours; those of the innermost planets must
endure perpetual and intense heat, while those of the outermost
experience the extremity of cold. Georgium sidus is the remotest of
all the planets, and is attended with two satellites or moons, the first
or nearest of which performs a synodical revolution in about 8 days
and 16 hours, and the second (which is about as far again distant
from its primary planet) in about 13 days and 12 hours. The moon
performs her course round the earth in about $29\frac{1}{2}$ days, and turns
round her own axis in nearly the same period: From the first of
these lunar motions we have the vicissitude of new and full moon,
for when she is between us and the sun, the dark side of her is next
the earth, so that she becomes invisible; and if in a right line with
him, she eclipses his light from us even in the day-time; but when
she is above or beyond the earth, she shews her full face to us,
which is called the full moon; and when the earth comes
immediately between these luminaries, she eclipses the reflecting

light of the moon from us, and the real light of the sun from the
lunarians, to whom the earth bears some relation similar to what
the moon does to us, only with this difference, that as the moon
goes round the earth, she is variously seen from every part of it in
each of her vicissitudes; but the earth not going round the moon,
though the full earth and new earth appear at the periods opposite
to our full moon and new moon, but few of the lunarians can see
them without travelling a great way for that purpose; and her diurnal motion being only at the rate of one revolution in 29½ days,
render it impossible to see the earth from every part of her surface
at once, or from any part of it more than once during that period.
She is once a year carried round the sun along with the earth. Many
of the fixed stars are supposed to be of the same matter with our
sun, and created for the same end or purpose, each of them the centre of its own proper system having planets revolving round it as
our sun has. Mr Fisher says, we have very narrow views of the
divine wisdom if we suppose the stars were made for no other end
than to give us a little dim light, for we receive more from the
moon than from them all put together. Comets are a sort of planets
that move in very eccentric orbits, moving almost directly towards
or from the sun; so that in their nearest approach, the heat must be
insupportable; and that heat exhaling a great deal of vapour in their
atmospheres, through which the sun's piercing rays are
immediately directed, causes the appearance of a long streaming
tail, having the resemblance of fire or smoke; and while they are in
their perihelion or nearest approach to the sun, they move more
rapidly, and their stay is shorter, on account of that rapidity; but
when they recede far from him, their motion becomes slower in
proportion to their distances, and are consequently longer before
they return: In this position they must experience a degree of cold
beyond conception: Some have even been bold enough to say that
h–ll is contained in them, from their exposure to such great
extremes of heat and cold.

Having thus given a very short view of the system of the
universe, I shall now proceed to give a more accurate and particular
description of this earth or planet on which we live; its dimensions,
various motions and connexions with other of the heavenly bodies
and various parts of the universe. It is a composition of land and
water of an almost spherical form, or rather an oblate figure, and

called the terraqueous globe from that very composition and form, although it be not a perfect sphere but rather flattish toward the poles, and resembles the shape of an orange. Before I proceed, it may be necessary to take notice, that the vast expanse which appears as a spacious concave or canopy whelmed over our heads, is only free space, in which all the heavenly bodies move by direction of him who first brought them into existence; and that beautiful azure under which clouds move, and in which the sun, moon, and stars are seen to appear, is no more than a boundary of our sight; for go where you may it has the same form and appearance, with only the variation of position, distant or nearer views of some of the different bodies which, as before observed, move in free and immense space, yet in such exact and regular order, that they never interfere or clash with each other, which might be prejudicial or even ruinous to some of them; as suppose Jupiter to strike against our earth, he would dash it to atoms. In order to ascertain the position of places, geographers have found it necessary to imagine certain circles drawn upon the surface of the earth, to which they have given the names of equator, meridian, horizon, parallels of latitude, &c. The equator is a great circle of the globe, which running from east to west, divides it into two almost equal parts, called the northern and southern hemispheres; parallel to the equator, are two other supposed circles called the tropics; the one north, which is called the tropic of cancer, and the other south, which is denominated the tropic of capricorn; each of these are 23 degrees, 29 minutes or miles distant from the plane of the equator; and parallel to these are two other circles, at the distance of 43 deg. 02 min. from the tropics, and each 23 deg. 29 min. from the poles; these are called the polar circles; the northermost the artic polar circle, and the southermost the antartic polar circle: The poles themselves are the two extreme points of the sphere, each of which are 90 deg. 00 min. from the equator, and 180 deg. 00 min. from each other; the artic or north pole is found by the pointers, seven stars so called, or vulgarly the wain; and the antartic or south pole is found by the crosiers, a small constellation of five stars, which do not appear till you come into latitude 17 deg. 00 min. north; and when you have run into about 17 deg. 00 min. of south latitude, you will run down or lose sight of the pointers; and thus by varying your position, you also vary the appearance of the asterial heavens, in respect to the direction and magnitude of the several bodies, but no more. The horizon is a transverse line or circle which gives bounds to our sight, and seems to divide between land and sky; or at sea, between water and sky; and the point immediately over head is called the zenith, and that directly under us the nadir, each of which are 90 deg. 00 min. from the horizon, one above and the other below. The meridian or mid-day circle is the sun's place at noon, and meridians are proper to every place on the face of the globe; they are circles crossing the equator at right angles, and dividing the earth into two equal parts, one east and the other west, and are so called because when the sun comes to the meridian of any place, it is then noon or mid-day there, but instantly changes and becomes noon on a more westerly meridian: And as each of these meridional lines are drawn through the zenith, nadir, and each of the poles, if you pursue it through either of them till you come to a latitude in the other hemisphere entirely in opposition to your own, that place is called the antipodes to that where you are, because there the seasons, &c. are opposite: It is as though you drew a line through the centre of the sphere, so that there mid-day will be midnight here, midsummer there midwinter here, and the longest day there the shortest day here: The antipodes to the city of London is part of the Pacific Ocean, in latitude 51 deg. 32 min. south, and longitude 180 deg. 00 min. either east or west, where the sun bears due north at noon, whereas he bears due south at London twelve hours before or after, so that consequently the shadow must fall quite the contrary way; and the length of night there is always in proportion to the length of day here. The earth is endued with a wonderful principle of gravitation, whereby all its parts are strictly united or caused to adhere together, and all bodies that are loose upon it closely press to its surface, tending directly to its centre: Hence it is that ships are able to sail with the same facility every where, if void of impediments, quite round the terraqueous globe; and that, with respect to sense, there is no such thing as upper and lower parts of the earth; for let the inhabitant be in what place soever he may, he will there gravitate toward the centre of the earth, and imagine himself to be on the highest point of the surface, from whence he will observe the heavens like a spacious canopy over his head, and his antipodes he will imagine to be directly under the earth, as they who are his antipodes or at the opposite part of the sphere will also, for the like reason, imagine exactly the same of his situation. Some suppose, that according to this law of gravity, if the earth were at rest and not acted upon by any other power, and its parts loose, or its surface covered all over with a deep fluid, it would naturally form itself into a sphere or globe; but admitting that the earth revolves round her own axis rapidly and continually, the gravity towards the centre will be disturbed by it, and all the parts endeavour to fly off from the axis of motion, and this inclination must be the greatest to that part of the surface which is at the greatest distance from the axis, and consequently the gravity towards the centre is there the least; whence it must follow, that those parts which gravitate the least must yield or give way to those that have a greater gravitation, to restore an equilibrium; and of course here will be formed a spheroid, whose greatest diameter will be perpendicular to the axis of the motion (commonly called the axis of the earth) and the shortest diameter will be the axis itself. The greatest diameter, which is under the equinoctial, is computed to be to the lesser diameter, which is under the poles or the earth's axis, as 289 to 288, and so consequently the space upon the earth's surface answering to a degree of a great circle, where it is the greatest, is to the space answering to a degree of a circle, where it is least, in so near a proportion, that in all astronomical and geographical cases, it may be considered as nothing, and the figure of the earth may be esteemed truly spherical, though the small difference may sensibly affect some things belonging to mechanicism. Add to this gravitation the compression of atmospheric air, for the earth is environed quite round her surface with an atmosphere or body of air, which presses every thing to it, and also exhilarates the life and motion of every aerial being, or such as cannot live without air. It likewise attracts water from the sea and exhalations from the ground, which form and fill the clouds, and the fluid there rarified, again descends in drops of rain whenever it becomes heavier than air, unless it congeals in its descent, and then it is hail or snow. When this atmospheric air is light, it not only suffers rain, &c. to fall, but so sensibly affects our bodies, that we feel heavy, faint, and inactive; for the heavier it presses on us, the more lightsome and active we feel. Some philosophers have supposed that about 600lbs weight of heterogeneous air lies on the body of every common sized person. Climates are certain spaces in which the day is increased or

lengthened half an hour; they are thirty in number in either hemisphere, and are much wider near the equator than they are when
you approach near the polar circles, which is occasioned by the
declivity of the earth's surface, and the oblique direction of the sun's
beams or rays, which determine each of these divisions in a direction parallel to the plane of the equator in right lines. – The afore
mentioned two causes vary the length of the artificial day from
twelve hours on the equinoctial to six months at each of the poles,
and give to each of the different parts of the globe an equal degree
of light in the course of the year, though not an equal degree of
heat. Latitude or breadth is taken from the equator, and known by
certain divisions called degrees and minutes or miles; a degree is 69½
English miles, but for the sake of readiness in reckoning, especially
keeping a journal at sea, the geographical mile is made use of,
which contains 2038 yards and two-thirds, 60 of which make a
degree, or 122320 yards equal to 69½ English miles. These lines
always running parallel to the equator, determine the situation of
any place lying north or south of it, and are of infinite use in keeping a reckoning at sea, to determine the northing and southing the
ship gains every day while at sea, which is found by use of the
quadrant, when the sun can be seen at 12 o'clock, or when he is on
the meridian, though an observation may be taken by other instruments and at other times, but not with so much accuracy: It is
measured by an arch of the meridian intercepted between any place
and the equator, and therefore can never exceed 90 deg. 00 min.
north or south; which denominations are derived from the situation of the place being either north or south of the equator;
therefore all places that lie on the same side of it, and at equal distance, are said to be under the same parallel of latitude; thus, the
Cape of Good Hope and Botany Bay are on a parallel of latitude
within half a degree, the former lying in 34 deg. 30 min. south, and
the latter in 34 deg. 00 min. ditto. All parallels of latitude are circles
encompassing the whole sphere, every part at equal distance from
the equator; and difference of latitude is an arch of the meridian
contained between two of those parallels, shewing how far one
place is to the northward or southward of another. – The greatest
difference of latitude cannot exceed 180 deg. 00 min. Some have
called the obscure and enlightened parts of the globe the upper and
lower hemispheres, and the equal parts contained between any

chief meridian and its antipodes they have called the eastern and western hemispheres; which definitions, though proper enough, are but seldom used to any necessary purpose. The Longitude or length is easting or westing, which is taken from or begun at some chief meridian, which thence is called the first meridian, and was formerly taken from that of Teneriffe; but it has of late years been the practice of navigators, to begin their longitude from the metropolis of the country or empire to which they respectively belong. The Dutch begin theirs at the meridian of Amsterdam; the French, from Paris; the Spaniards, from Madrid, or else Cape Finistere; the Portuguese, from the rock of Lisbon, &c. and we, instead of the Lizard, now take it either from London or Greenwich. A degree of longitude on the equator is equal to a degree of latitude, 60 geographic miles, but diminishes as you recede from it, at first very gradually till you begin to raise your latitude to about 30 deg. 00 min. and then more rapidly till it terminates in nothing at the pole, where all the meridians coincide. This gradation in the length of a degree of longitude the judicious navigator must carefully allow for, in the proportionate length of his miles of longitude, as it is always necessary to account 60 miles to a degree, for the sake of readiness and exactness in keeping a reckoning. The difference of longitude between the above places is 133 deg. 48 min. Some may think that speaking of the length of a globular figure is a kind of ambiguity; I allow it; but it is used in contradistinction to latitude, as no fitter word is known for that purpose. The longitude of any place on the earth is expressed by an arch of the equator, shewing the east or west distance of the meridian of that place from some fixed meridian where longitude is reckoned to begin: And difference of longitude is an arch of the equator intercepted between the meridians of two places, shewing how far one of them is to the eastward or westward of the other. As longitude begins at some place or grand meridian, and is counted from thence both eastward and westward till it meets at the same meridian on the opposite point, therefore the difference of longitude can never exceed 180 deg. 00 min. or a semicircle of the globe; though a navigator, proceeding either east or west round it, may continue his account by east or west longitude, till he arrives at the port sailed from, when he will have accumulated 360 deg. 00 min. of east or west longitude without any false reckoning or impropriety. When a ship is on the equator, both the poles appear in the horizon; and in proportion as she sails towards either, or increases her latitude, that pole is seen proportionably above the horizon, and the other disappears as much; but when a ship is sailing towards the line, or decreases her latitude, she depresses the elevated pole so as to bring it nearer the horizon; so that the latitude of a place may be found by the elevation of the pole above the horizon of that place, it being equal thereto: And was it possible for a ship to be at either of the poles, the equator would then be her true horizon; which circle, as it becomes proper to any and every part of the globe, is fitly represented by the mariner's compass, which is divided into 32 rhumbs or points, each 11 deg. 15 min. The tropics and polar circles divide the world into five zones, three of which have in some ages been thought uninhabitable, from their intemperance in the degrees of heat and cold – as much might be thought of Mercury and Jupiter. These divisions called zones are distinguished by the names of torrid or hot, temperate, and frigid or frozen zones. The torrid zone is contained between the two tropics, and is 46 deg. 58 min. in breadth; this is by far the largest, and at the two extremes of it the sun is vertical or over-head once a year, and in all other parts of it, twice; so that his direct or perpendicular beams dart straight down on an erect object at noon, so as to leave it no shadow, although in the course of the year it falls every way, sometimes north at noon and sometimes south; for as the sun's greatest declination from the equinoctial reaches to the tropics alternately, he must pass over the heads of those who live within those circles, and cause the shadow to fall the contrary way at noon; and when he repasses them, it falls in an opposite direction. In this zone the degrees of heat are never very sensibly abated, because there is never so much obliquity in the direction of the sun's rays through the atmosphere as to make any material or even very perceptible difference, or any great variation in the vegetation of the ground, which will produce at any time of the year if favoured with rains; nor of the trees, which have a perpetual verdure, for some or other of them bear fruit at all seasons of the year. The two temperate zones are contained between the tropics and the polar circles, and are each 43 deg. 02 min. in breadth; in these zones only we can with propriety say there is summer and winter, and these are very different at or near the extremes, with respect to severity and mildness; for near their innermost or first

limits, they partake much of the nature of the middle or torrid
zone; and where they border on the frigid zone, they are very
nearly allied to its extreme cold, especially while the sun is in the
opposite tropical sign, when they have scarcely any day; and even in
the middle parts of these zones there is much difference on the
same parallels of latitude, occasioned by the nature of the several
countries respecting the variety of the soil and humidity or dryness
of atmosphere, as in America, some parts of which are full of large
fresh water lakes, rivers, and swamps, which make it as cold in latitude 40 as in some parts of Europe in 50 deg. And throughout the
southern hemisphere, the cold is found to exceed what it is mostly
in the northern on the several parallels of opposite latitudes. In our
zone the shadow falls north, and in the southern temperate zone it
falls south at noon, each veering round from west to east, for those
who live under the same meridians but on opposite parallels; they
having the sun at noon in a contrary direction, and their seasons
different, so that their summer is our winter and their winter our
summer, and their longest day is our shortest day, &c. but their
noon and midnight perfectly correspond with ours, so that in this
only they differ from those who are antipodes to each other, whose
mid-days and mid-nights are opposite, and their feet directed
against the feet of those who stand or walk on the other side of the
sphere. But on account of the vicissitudes of heat and cold, the
natives and residents of these zones (by the densation and rarification of the blood) are subjected to a greater variety of acute and
chronical diseases than those of the torrid zone, whose blood being
at a constant flow, and many of them living very temperate, are in
general more healthy and live to greater ages than those who are at
one season of the year shivering with cold and at another oppressed
with heat; and again at intervals between these extremes, they are
temperate. The frigid zones encompass the poles to which they
respectively belong at the distance of 23 deg. 29 min. and beginning
at 66 deg. 31 min. from the equator, where the longest day is 24
hours, being double to what it is there; for when the sun has north
declination, the farther you recede from the equator northward the
longer the day; so on the contrary, when he has south declination,
the farther you leave the equator to the southward the more you
will increase the length of the day, whereas at the equator it is
never more than 12 hours from sunrising to sunsetting, or what is

sometimes called an artificial day. Those who live in the frigid zones are called Perisians, because their shadow falls quite round them in a circular form: Those who inhabit the other two opposite temperate zones are called Hetresians, because their seasons are neither extremely hot nor intensely cold, and their shadows fall contrary ways: And those who dwell in the middle zone are nominated Amphisians, from the direction of their vortex or shadow as before mentioned. The sphere at the poles being entire fluid, there is a natural propensity in that element to fly off by the earth's diurnal motion, which disposition is checked by freezing, and made impossible by the compression of atmospheric air, yet it certainly must cause a flatness at the poles; and as the equator is their true horizon when the sun is in either equinox, so when the sun has entered Aries and gained so much north declination as, if viewed from the artic pole, would shew him quite above the horizon, he immediately shines through, past, and round the said pole, so as to make it entire day as far as 5 deg. 55 min. and in proportion as his declination increases, so his rays reach farther and farther into the other hemisphere, until they reach the polar circle on the opposite meridian, which makes each of these zones 46 deg. 58 min. wide or broad; for when the sun is in Cancer, the pole is elevated 23 deg. 29 min. and the tropic becomes the horizon to the Artic Circle in 180 deg. 00 min. difference of longitude; and if viewed from thence at midnight, the sun appears in the horizon as if rising or setting. Here the longest day is from 1 to 6 months; as from the sun's entering the 15th degree of Gemini to his reaching the 15th degree of Cancer, constitutes the longest day in the 25th climate between 66 deg. 31 min. and 67 deg. 21 min. and from his entering Gemini to his entering Leo, makes the longest day in the 26th climate between 67 deg. 21 min. and 69 deg. 48. min. so from his advancing to the 15th degree of Taurus to his receding to the 15th of Leo, makes the longest day in the 27th climate between 69 deg. 48 min. and 73 deg. 37 min, and from his entering Taurus to his entering Virgo, makes the longest day in the 28th climate between 73 deg. 37 min. and 78 deg. 30 min. so from his gaining the 15th degree of Aries to his reaching the 15th of Virgo, makes the longest day in the 29th climate between 78 deg. 30 min. and 84 deg. 05 min. so likewise the time he is in the northern hemisphere constitutes the longest day in the 30th or extreme climate, which is 6 months; the next, 5 months;

next to that, 1 months; next to that, 3 months; next to that, 2 months; and the other, 1 month. The shadow here falls every way in 24 hours, as it is varied quite round in that time; it falls due north at noon and due south at midnight, the sun being then on the opposite meridian and shining through the pole; but it does not fall due west at 6 in the morning, nor due east at 6 in the evening, but inclines northerly in proportion to the sun's zenith distance: Observe the length of it varies much. Again, when the sun has entered Libra and gained south declination enough to raise his lower disk above the horizon when viewed from the Antartic pole, his rays then reach through it as far as 5 deg. 55 min. which they continue to illuminate for 6 months, till he recedes back to the first degree of Aries; this makes the longest day in the 30th climate; and from his entering the 15th degree of Libra, to his receding back to the 15th of Pisces, makes the longest day in the 29th climate; from his entering into Scorpio to his entering into Pisces, makes the longest day in the 28th climate; from his gaining 15 deg. 00 min. in Scorpio to his receding back 15 deg. 00 min. in Aquarius, makes the longest day in the 27th climate; from his entering Sagittarius to his returning to enter Aquarius, makes the longest day in the 26th climate; from his advancing 15 deg. 00 min. in Sagittarius to his receding 15 deg. 00 min. in Capricornus, makes the longest day in the 25th climate; the length of each day corresponding with those of the northern hemisphere. The mid-day at the south pole is when the sun enters into Capricorn, and midnight when he enters into Cancer. Here the shadow falls in every direction in 24 hours, but contrary to the directions in which it falls in the northern zone; for as there it falls due north at noon and veers round easterly till it falls due south at 12 o'clock at night, so here it falls due south at noon and veers round easterly till it comes to fall due north at midnight, the sun being then on the opposite meridian and shining through the pole as before observed. In those climates where they have a day of 1, 2, 3, 4, 5, or 6 months long, they have an equal degree of night including their twilight, and at the other seasons of the year they have the vicissitudes of day and night, sunrise and sunset, &c. though then their night is chiefly twilight if not altogether so, as the light reaches farther round in proportion as the circumference becomes less, until it enlightens the whole circuit, whereas the aurora is of very short duration in low latitudes. The miserable inhabitants of these inhospitable zones, as they experience a total absence of the sun, and never see him have any great altitude, so they hardly ever feel any comfortable degree of natural heat; and were not their constitutions robust and hardy, and so adapted by nature to those climates, they could not live in them, as is evident from the experiments that have been made by the Dutch and Rusians who attempted to winter in Greenland, and perished in that attempt. The country is always covered with ice and snow. The equinoctial line of the celestial sphere is a circle which corresponds with the equator of the terrestrial globe, and from thence they are confounded sometimes when spoken of indefinitely, as if they meant one and the same thing. The ecliptic is the ellipsis in which the earth moves round the sun, which cutting the equinoctial in right angles at the two points called nodes or equinoxes, about the 21st of March and 22d of September, (when there is equal day and night in every part of the globe) by varying the direction of the sun's perpendicular rays as she passes under the twelve signs of the zodiac variously and indifferently, brings every part of the torrid zone directly under them: And this annual motion of the earth is the cause of the various seasons of spring, summer, autumn, and winter, which are not the effect of her nearer approach to or farther receding from the sun, but from her varying her position in the ecliptic, so called from the afore mentioned cutting of the line at the nodes; for in reality the earth is nearer to the sun in either summer or winter, than when she is in either the vernal or autumnal equinox, her orbit being an ellipsis, which is also the reason why the sun's declination is every day greater when he is on or near the line, than when he is either in Cancer or Capricorn, although the earth's motion be equally rapid, her course being then more directly north or south; and hence the length of the day is increased faster in March than in June. I shall illustrate this by a comparison — Suppose a ship sails at any certain rate, having taken her departure from a place on the equator, and steers N. N. W. several days; then varies her course to N. W. by N. then again to N. W. and next to N. W. by W. it is certain her northing, by the first of these courses, will be greater than by the second; and by her third course, only equal to her westing; and by the last mentioned course, her northing will be to her westing only as 3 to 5 as she comes more into a right line; yet it is presumed she has run in these several directions with an equal degree of velocity, which must be true respecting the annual motion of the earth round the sun, which is at the rate of 58000 miles an hour, and performed in 365 days, 5 hours, 48 minutes, and 55 seconds, or what we call a year, or one revolution of the earth round the sun, as her proper centre. The zodiac is a part of the ethereal heavens contained between two parallels of the celestial sphere, which are correspondent to those on the terrestrial, which we call the tropics, in which space is contained the twelve constellations, known by the character of the signs of the zodiac, the names of which are Aries, Taurus, Gemini, Cancer, Leo, Virgo, Libra, Scorpio, Sagittarius, Capricornus, Aquarius, and Pisces. As the sun enters one of these signs, the earth always enters into its opposite, and passes through it in an equal period of time. The axis is a supposed or imaginary line drawn through the centre of the earth from pole to pole, which are each others' antipodes, and is called the axis from the simile of a wheel turning on an axle-tree, thereby to represent the earth's diurnal motion, which is from west to east, in the space of 24 hours, which is an astronomical or natural day, beginning at noon, which beginning of time is always used in keeping a journal at sea: This motion, though it could not be perceived at the poles, is at the rate of $1042\frac{1}{2}$ English miles, which is equal to 900 nautical or geographical miles, an hour; so that by this, the circumference of the sphere being 25020 English or 21600 nautical miles, it must follow, that every 15 degrees easting or westing make an hour of time; so if you go 15 degrees eastward, you will have it noon there when it is only 11 o'clock on the meridian you have left; and if you proceed 15 degrees westward, you will then have it noon when it is 1 o'clock at the place you left; and this will hold as well near the poles, where all the meridians coincide, as on the equator, where 15 degrees are 900 miles: Observe 1 degree makes 4 minutes; 15 miles, 1 minute; and 1 mile, 4 seconds; so that the difference of longitude between two places being known, it is easy to determine their different times of day. I shall endeavour to make this doctrine of the earth's diurnal motion plain to any capacity, by a simple comparison – Suppose you run a wire through an apple and place it before the fire; while you hold it still, only one side will roast or be illuminated; but if you keep turning it round, the whole will be heated and enlightened. This diurnal moving of the sphere round its own axis from west to east is the cause of the vicissitudes of light, twilight, and darkness; for when the sun appears in the eastern horizon, we call it sunrise, and when he has come to the meridian of the place where we are, it is noon; so when he comes to disappear in the western horizon, we say it is sunset, and twilight commences and continues until he is 18 degrees below it, when we call it night; and when he is come to the meridian opposite to ours, it is midnight; so likewise when he arrives within 18 deg. of the eastern horizon again, the aurora or morning twilight begins: Thus are we whirled quite round almost imperceptibly in the course of ever natural day. I shall illustrate this assertion by an example – Suppose two ships, one called the *Asia* and the other the *America*, sail from Plymouth and keep company till they arrive at the island of Trinidad on the coast of South America, and there separate, and the *Asia* to fail E. by S. till she passes Van Dieman's land, or else make the Cape of Good Hope, and taking a fresh departure thence, steers E. $\frac{1}{2}$ S. till she makes the little islands of St. Paul and Amsterdam, in latitude about 39 deg. 20 min. south, and longitude 77 deg. 12 min. east; then haul up N.E. across the trade wind, and pass through some of the straits of Malacca, or those of Sunda and Banca, &c. into the Pacific Ocean; and as soon as she is got clear of all the islands, shape her course towards the antipodes of London: And the *America* to coast along the shores of Brazil, Paraguay, Patagonia, and Magellenica, and so either pass through the straits of Magellan or else round Cape Horn on the southern extremity of Terra-del-Fuego, into the great Pacific Ocean likewise, (allowing her here to meet with blowing weather and contrary winds so as to retard her passage and give the other ship time) so that each pursuing her route, they at length meet in the antipodes, or on some other part of the grand meridian, 180 deg. 00 min. east by the *Asia*'s account, and west by that of the *America*'s; when the former will have gained 12 hours, and the latter will have lost 12; so that if it was Sunday by the *Asia*'s reckoning, it would be only Saturday by the *America*'s: Then having spoke with each other and enquired about their most remarkable occurrences, &c. let each pursue her voyage round the world till they again meet in Plymouth Sound; the ship which has sailed east about will have gained a day, and the other which sailed west about will have lost a day; yet each shall have kept a just and correct reckoning; and supposing them to arrive on the 6th of July at noon, it will, by the *Asia*'s journal, be the 7th, and by that of the

America only the 5th day of the same month. This is a certain proof
of the earth's motion round her own axis, which has been verified
by all the circumnavigators who have at different times sailed
round the globe; the first of which was the Portuguese Admiral
Magellan, then Thomas Cavendish, and next Sir Francis Drake;
afterwards Commodore Anson; and since that, Byron, Cateret,
Wallis, Bouganville, Fourneaux, Cook, Clarke, Dixon, Hamilton,
&c. &c. some of whom have sailed east and others west about. How
much easier is it for the earth to revolve round her own axis by her
own gravity, than for the sun, whose diameter is 763000 miles, to go
round her in 24 hours, at the rate of 211840531 miles an hour. With
respect to the correspondence of time with the seasons, or the
length of time in which the earth performs her revolution round
the sun, much labour has been used to determine: In the first ages
of the world, both before and after the deluge, they kept lunar time,
and calculated their year from the moon's age; and to make their
seasons correspondent thereto, they added a certain space of time to
make up the defect, and thereby correct their style, which required
to be done frequently and by various methods, making every 3d
year 13 moons, and every 21st and 22d years long-years. The
Chaldean astronomers at length found that the earth revolved
round the sun as her centre, and began to compute by solar time,
allowing 30 deg. 00 min. to each sign of the zodiac, and so making
the year to consist of only 360 days, which was very deficient: This
took place, as some think, in the patriarchal age. To remedy the
defect, the Egyptians, in the reign of Ptolomy, anno mundi, 2272,
added 5 days, calling them epagomona or superadded, by which
they constituted the year of 365 days: This calculation also being
found defective, the Romans, in the reign of Julius Cæsar, added 6
hours, which became an excess of 11 minutes and 5 seconds; the
year being, by minute attention and strict observation, found to be
365 days, 5 hours 48 minutes, and 55 seconds. And as by the calculation according to the Julian or old style, the odd 6 hours were
reckoned but once in four years, to avoid fractions, and that year
accounted to contain 366 days, from whence it was called the bis-
sextile, (a year of double-six, or vulgarly the leap-year) because then
remarkable days leapt over a day of the week; but by this allowance
we must account every leap-year 44 minutes and 20 seconds longer
than it really is: And the earth having passed the node so long

before the expiration of the time fixed, (as the integral of the year) has proceeded according to the allowed extent of her orbit or track 42851½ miles on her way towards another revolution; so that in the year 325, the earth was observed to enter the first point of Libra on the 21st of March; but in the year 1582, it was observed to enter it on the 11th of March; wherefore Pope Gregory the XIII caused 10 days to be left out in October, accounting the 5th to be the 15th; which regulation was adopted in most of the nations of Europe; and at last in Great Britain in the year 1752, when, by the authority of the legislature, 11 days were left out of the British calendar, and September the 3d was reckoned the 14th. This caused much rumour and speculation amongst illiterate people. To prevent the necessity of so large a reform in future, the following method is now adopted by all the nations and empires of Europe, viz. to leave out 3 days in the course of every 400 years, to take place from the year 1600; so that the years 1800 and 1900, which should be leap-years, will be accounted common years, but the year 2000 will be a leap-year; so also the years 2100, 2200, and 2300, will be reckoned as common years, but 2400 will be a leap-year. This will keep time, and the seasons nearly, though not exactly correspondent; for as a day is gained by the fraction of time in 129 years, 337 days, 18 hours, 43 minutes, and 53 seconds, 3 days being left out in 400 years, will leave 10 years, 27 days, 11 hours, 5 minutes, and 2 seconds, for which the fraction 11 minutes and 5 seconds have not been reckoned, the sum of which is 1 hour, 53 minutes, and 20 seconds; but this will not amount to a day in less than 5082 years, 128 days, 21 hours, 49 minutes, and 2 seconds; so that the true necessity of leaving out 2 days together is what may never happen while the world endures. The real parts of the globe are earth and water, generally divided into four parts or quarters, called Europe, Asia, Africa, and America; each of these, and of consequence the whole sphere, is divided into continents, islands, seas, rivers, &c. the terrestrial part of the sphere is composed of continents, islands, peninsulas, isthmuses, capes, points, &c. The three continents of Europe, Asia, and Africa, are large tracts of land not bounded by the sea so as to separate them from any other, or one dominion from another; nay these three are connected one with another, for the two former join together, so that they might well enough be called one continent divided into empires and states; and Africa is joined to Asia by the

isthmus of Suez, so that travellers may go from Egypt into Arabia
without crossing the water. America indeed is a separate continent,
and from its being so far detached from the other continents, as
well as its being later found out, has been called the New World;
and some have even conjectured that it escaped the deluge, because
Columbus, the first European discoverer of it, found much of it
inhabited, and could not tell how such inhabitants could come
there, unless they had continued in succession from the Creation.
The principal islands are as follows: Great Britain, though but very
small in comparison to some, in point of eminence far exceedeth
them, and being my native country, I shall therefore place her
first, although New Holland is by far the largest island in the
world. Some other of the chief islands are Borneo, Japan, Sumatra,
Java, Madagascar, Otaheite, California, Formosa, New Zealand,
Terra-del-Fuego, Ceylon, Cuba, Hispaniola, Jamaica, Martinico,
Gaudalope, Ireland, Sicily, Newfoundland, &c. The principal capes
are the Cape of Good Hope, Horn, Florida, Comorin, Finisterre,
North Cape, Naize, &c. which are sometimes spoken of for
their eminence, as if there were no others, yet there are many hundreds more of less note, such as Cape Cornwall, Cape-de-Verd,
Cape Three-points, &c. The aqueous part consists of oceans, seas,
lakes, bays, gulfs, straits, rivers, races, channels, &c. The oceans are
the Atlantic, Pacific, and Indian; the German sea too is called an
ocean; and sometimes the South sea, contained between the meridian of the cape and the eastern shore of South America, is called the
South Atlantic ocean. The principal seas are the Mediterranean,
Baltic, Greenland, White, and China seas; which last are a part of
the Pacific Ocean. The chief lakes are Lake Ontario, Lake
Champlain, Lake George, the Lake of Geneva, &c. The bays of
most eminence are those of Biscay, Bengal, Honduras, Campeachy,
&c. which are extensive parts of the sea that are surrounded with
the shore all but on one side. The principal gulfs are those of
Florida, Mexico, St Lawrence, Finland, Lyons, Venice, Persia, and
Arabia, with several others of less note, such as the gulf of Adria,
&c. I have often heard country people talk much about shooting the
gulf, and the very absurd notions they entertained about it; some of
them supposing it to be some unaccountable strange place or passage, the passing of which ushered them into another world, or at
least brought them under this; and some have conceived, that the

ship must go head foremost, or they know not how, down some whirlpool or gullyhole, like Harlequin going into a bottle. The straits of most note are those of Gibraltar, Magellan, Malacca, Sunda, Banca, and Davis'. The principal rivers in point of eminence and magnitude are the Thames, Humber, Elbe, Rhine, Weser, Scheld, Volga, Seine, Tigris, Ganges, Indus, Nile, Niger, Bolcharica, Rio-de-la Plata, Rio-Grande, Ohio, Mississippi, St Lawrence, Amazon, Cook's River, &c. An island is a part of the earth which is entirely surrounded by the sea so as to cut it off from any other land, such as Great Britain or her sister kingdom. A peninsula differs from an island by being joined to a continent or other land by a narrow neck, which is called an isthmus, as North and South America are joined together by the isthmus of Darien between Porto-Bello and Panama. A promontory is a very high part of land which stretches out into the sea, the extremity of which we call a cape, headland, or cliff. A mountain is a very high hill in an interior part of the country overtopping the other parts, and that may be seen first at a distance, like the highland of St Martha in South America. A point is a part of low land projecting into the sea. The earth being environed with water, whose various washings surround the dry land, cut and shape a variety of bays, creeks, and inlets, and extending itself round them all, is properly but one ocean, which yet is known by several denominations as if it were many. The northern ocean is contained between the N. W. shores of Asia and the N. E. parts of America, lying north of Great Britain, Norway, Lapland, Finland, and Russia, including the White Sea. The Atlantic is contained between Europe and North America, east and west, having Africa on the south, and is often called the western ocean; the other part of it, as before observed, is contained between the south coast of Africa and the south pole and west of the Cape of Good Hope. The Indian Ocean extends from the meridian of the cape to the Sonda islands and the west end of New Holland. And the Pacific Ocean is comprehended between the eastern shores of the afore mentioned islands and that of the continent of Asia and the western shores of South and North America, and is divided at the equator into the south and north Pacific or peaceful ocean, as its atmospheres have not so frequently resounded the echos of naval thunder as the European seas. What is called a sea is a part of the vast ocean that is chiefly encompassed with land, except at a narrow entrance, as the Mediterranean, which is bounded on the north by Spain, part of France, Genoa, Leghorn, Italy, the kingdom of Naples, and part of Turkey; on the east by Turkey and some part of Arabia, and on the south by Egypt, Tunis, part of Morocco, and Algiers; and the Baltic, which is included between the shores of Sweden, Finland, Russia, Poland, Prussia, and Denmark. The Black and Caspian seas are each little more than fresh water lakes. A lake is a very extensive quantity of fresh water contained in an interior cavity of the earth that receives and retains it, or discharges it into some river or rivers which convey what it is surcharged with into the ocean. The lake Zaire in Africa, and the lakes Parana, Nicaragua, and Ontario in America, are very extensive; the latter of which is 100 leagues in length and 80 in breadth, discharging its extraneous waters into the great rivers Mississippi and St Lawrence, through different outlets. A gulf is either a deep bay, as the gulfs of Mexico and Finland, or the wide entrance into a river, as those of St Lawrence and La-Plata; the former of which is 25 leagues, and the latter 100 miles broad at the entrance; or an inlet of the sea, such as the gulfs of Persia and Arabia; the latter of which is often called the Red Sea, from the colour of the sand at the bottom, which when violently agitated, gives the water an apparent tinge; or else a strait with a very rapid stream running between two headlands, as the gulf of Florida, where it runs so impetuously, that vessels falling into it in a calm, have been drove as far as the banks of Newfoundland before they could get clear of it; and on the contrary, when the wind blows strong from the northward, by which it is made a windward current, it is frequently so rough that it is sufficient to dash an old crazy vessel to pieces. We say a vessel is ingulfed when she has got into an intricate situation amongst rocks, &c. A strait is a narrow passage into a sea that is land-locked, or a communication between one part of the ocean and another, as the Straits of Gibraltar and that called the Sound, which is the passage into the Baltic, and lies between Sweden and Denmark: And those of the latter description are such as the strait between the south Foreland and Calais clifts; also those that lead through the asiatic Archipelago into the China seas, such as Pitt's straits, and that between Terra-del-Fuego and the southern extremity of South America, known by the name of Magellan. Davis' and Behring's straits indeed are different from any of the former, being only difficult passages amongst ranges of rocks, &c. the former of these being situated on the eastern shore of America between 62 and 71 degrees of north latitude, and the latter on the western shore washed by the Pacific Ocean on about the middle parallels of those latitudes. A race is a place where two opposite tides or strong currents meet and oppose each other so as to cause a violent but short irregular motion, which will sometimes stagnate the way of a ship, and fill or overset a boat. A channel is so well known that I need say nothing about it more than that it generally means the bed of a river, or a curve wrought by the force of a current between two sand-banks, &c. so as to make it passable for ships or vessels; and some of the lesser sort of channels are called creeks, though that more properly means an inlet of the sea. The Channel, lying between England and France, is so eminent and of such great national utility, that it is often distinguished by the name of King's channel, because the King's ports border on it; hence the fleet appointed for home service is called the Channel Fleet. The Irish, or St George's channel, lies between the two sister kingdoms, and that called Bristol-channel branches out of it. The flux and reflux of the waters, which are called the tides of ebb and flood, are caused by the attraction and refraction of the sun and moon acting regularly and forcibly on the surface of the sea in a manner I shall not attempt to define, as it has employed the abilities of Sir Isaac Newton and other scientific gentlemen: I shall only observe, that the force of the tides are much greater in some places than in others; as in some rivers the tides are so very rapid, that when their force is strengthened by a strong gale of wind blowing in the same direction, it becomes necessary to steer ships at their anchor, to keep them stem on; for if they fall athwart the stream, they must either bring their anchors home, or perhaps overset. In the River Thames it would be impossible sometimes to stem either ebb or flood, if it was not for the meandering of the river, which is so serpentine, that there is only one point of the compass that the wind can be at, which will carry a ship from sea-reach into the pool without making a board, i. e. putting her about. The river St Lawrence too has very strong and rapid tides, which run at the rate of 9 or 10 knotts on the flood at spring tide, and 11 or 12 on the ebb, when joined by the fall of the fresh after-rains or melting of snow; and at the neaps it is hard to stem the tide. The waters of these two rivers are the best for using or carrying to sea of any I ever met with in the world. It must follow, that these agitations of the waters in the rivers have their sources from the sea washing the shores where they fall into it; but out at sea at some considerable distance from the land, a regular flowing of the tide is scarce perceptible, and indeed in many places there is none: In the Mediterranean there is very little, nor yet in the Baltic; so that large ships built at Petersburg are conveyed down to Cronstadt in camels, i.e. vases made to sink under their bottoms, and when pumped dry, they bear them above their proper draught of water; and in the West Indies, the want of tides render it necessary to heave ships down instead of docking them. But where there is little or no tide, there is often a strong current that sets variously in different parts of the seas, which great variety has many and different causes: They are sometimes caused by the remnant of tides ushering from between projecting lands that forbid their return; in other places, by the collected force of many streams of fresh water falling into the sea where there is not tide sufficient to interrupt their progress; and also from the winds having blown hard and long from one quarter of the compass: All these and some other causes contribute to make the setting and strength of currents various, and sometimes dangerous; from whence it becomes necessary to try them often at sea; in order to which, we hoist out a boat, and take in her a compass, a log, and an iron pot; and when she is out of the wake of the ship, put the pot overboard (it being properly slung for that purpose) and the concave of it will hold water so as to moor the boat, which tending with her head to the stream, will shew by the compass what way it sets; and by heaving the log, we find how fast it runs. The currents are partly caused, and their velocity greatly increased, by the two trade winds, within the compass of their reach on either side the equator; for these constantly blowing a stiff gale from the eastward, keep continually driving a weight of water to leeward; and where it is not obstructed by the land projecting out into the ocean, the water collects a force sufficient to form it into a current, and thus rolling through the Ethiopic sea down to the coast of Amazonia, and along between the Caribbee islands and the main land of South America, till it passes all the Leeward islands also; and the vast confluence of aqueous fluid thus collected, flows down into the bays of Honduras and Campeachy, where being brought up or stopped by the land, it takes a turn to the northward into the bay of Mexico, where it is joined by the stream falling out of the Mississippi, and flows along the shores of the two Floridas till it falls into the gulf of Florida, which runs between the N. W. point of Cuba and Cape Florida on the continent: And the narrowness of the bounds between the two lands, in proportion to the width of the ingress, is the chief cause of the rapidity of the Gulf Stream. As I have mentioned the trade winds, it may be necessary for me to say a few words concerning winds, which are currents of air variously acted upon. Notwithstanding the attractive power of gravitation to the centre of the earth, the sun's rays upon the surface cause vapors or fumes to be rising continually from it, which must partake of the quality of those parts from whence they are evaporated, a collection of which form what is called the atmosphere, which surrounds the earth, and extends some miles above it, and is liable to be put in motion from a number of different causes; hence it must follow, that air is a fine elastic fluid, and capable of compression or condensity by cold, and expansion or rarification by the contrary: And consequently, on an alteration in the degrees of heat or cold in any part of the atmosphere, the air in that part will be varied, and the neighbouring parts will be thereby put in motion through the endeavour which the air, by its elasticity or bounding disposition, always makes to restore itself to its former state, or come to an equal balance. Wind certainly is a current or stream of air, and generally blows from one part of the horizon towards its opposite, yet I have seen two ships standing one way close hauled, with the contrary tacks on board, which shewed 12 points difference in the direction of the wind. Where winds are variable, (as they are in most parts) they, by blowing and shifting, cause great vicissitudes in the currents, both with respect to their strength and directions; but between the latitudes of 5 deg. north and 5 south, there is frequently a dead calm and heavy rains, so that ships have lain several days without any way more than what was effected by the currents. Between latitude 5 and 27 or 28 deg. north, the wind always blows from about E. N. E. with little variation, when its course is not altered by the land breezes near any shore; and from 5 degrees south latitude to 27 or 28, it constantly blows from E. S. E. or nearly so, unless impeded as before mentioned: Those we call the trade winds; the former of which is called the N. E. trade, and the latter the S. E. trade, from the constant dependance we have on them in navigating these seas. The philosophical reasons of these winds I shall leave to the leisure and abilities of men of science, and only take notice, that the sun's rays heating the ground and exhaling vapors from it, which generate into winds (where there is either a continent or an island of considerable extent) they collect so much strength as to oppose the current of the trade wind or sea breeze, and blowing off shore, are called land breezes; and at certain times these different currents of air meet in such a variety of oblique and different directions, each of which oppose the other, that their fury is increased into a storm, which will sometimes veer from point to point, and frequently quite round the compass, in a few minutes. These gusts and whirlwinds are called hurricanes in the West Indies, where they generally happen in August, September, or October, though not every year, when they will blow down houses, tear trees up by the roots, dismast ships at sea, and bear down all before them. In the East Indies they call them monsoons, where they fall variously in different places, accordingly as the sun is vertical, and other concurrent causes determine. And on the coast of Africa they are termed tornadoes, where they are no less violent; for they often succeed a dead clam without any previous signs, from whence they do considerable hurt; whereas in the West Indies they mostly know how to prepare for them, as the wind will veer and haul 3 or 4 points, and dark confused clouds appear for some time before. The winds blowing hard at S. W. and S. W. by S. in the southern Atlantic during some of their winter months, force such a body of water round the east end of Madagascar, that it there falling into the current caused by the S. E. trade, so increases its force, that it sets down between that island and the main, and so becomes a windward current round the Cape of Good Hope, and will carry a ship round it when she is put past the use of her sails and laid to drive, as the harder it blows from these points the more force it gives to the current.

The following question was propounded to me by a gentleman on board the *Elizabeth*, while on her passage through the Indian Ocean in July, 1762, I gave it the working and proof, which I now submit to the inspection of my readers; and if any of them can give a better solution of it, I am very ready to pay a deference to their superior genius: And though a question of such a nature and magnitude may appear useless, yet I hope none will censure it, either because he cannot comprehend it, or won't be at the trouble to determine whether it is right or wrong.

> *If the terraqueous globe was a plane and a perfect sphere, how many solid or cubic inches would it contain?*

In answer to this, it is first necessary to adjust the difference between an English and a geographical mile, as the geographical mile is always used in navigation. I say then as $69\frac{1}{2}$ statute miles make a degree, (each such mile containing 1760 yards) how many yards make a geographical mile?

$$
\begin{array}{ccc}
\text{As } 69\frac{1}{2} & : \ 1760 \ :: & 60 \\
\underline{\ \ 2\ \ } & \underline{\ \ 139\ \ } & \underline{\ \ 2\ \ } \\
139 & 15840 & 120 \\
 & 5280 & \\
 & \underline{1760\ \ } & \\
12.0) & \underline{24464,0\ \ } & \\
 & 2038 \,,\, 2 & \\
\end{array}
$$

I shall not insert the whole working, but only the several results or products of the work, with the answer and its proof, leaving it to any mathematician to prove, or disprove if he please.

But I must observe, that there is contained in a square foot, 144 inches; in a yard, 9 feet; in an English mile, 3097600 yards; in a geographical mile, 4156161 yards and 7 square feet; in a cubic foot, 1728 inches; in a yard, 27 feet; in an English mile, 5451776000 yards; and in a geographical mile, 8473028477 yards and 17 single cubic feet.

I now state my question, and say, As 22 to 7, so is the circumference to the diameter; and then reduce from one denomination to another till I come to the lowest, and then multiply the circumference by the diameter, and that product is the area or superficial content. I again multiply by the one-sixth part of the diameter, and it gives the amplitude or solidity required.

Circumference of the globe in inches,   1585267200
Diameter, – – – – – – – – 504403200
Area, – – – – – – 799613848535040000

Answer in solid inches:

6722129732756491468800000

Thus proved, As 21 to 11, so is the cube of the diameter to the solid content.

```
                              504403200
                               504403200
                             100880640000
                             1513209600
                             2017612800
                             2017612800
                             2522016000
                           254422588170240000
                                       504403200
                           50884517634048000000
                           763267764510720000
                          10176903526809600000
                          10176903526809600000
                          12721129408512000000
                          128331567625351200768000000
                                                   11
  7)      14116472438788632084480000000
  3)      201663891982694744064000000
  21      6722129732756491468800000
```

Some give another way of working such questions, viz. by multiplying the cube of the diameter by this decimal, 5236, but it is not true; and though in a globe of small dimension the difference is but trifling, yet in such as this it is very material; in a globe of only 21 inches diameter, the defect is 2 inches; in one of 84 inches diameter, it will be 125 inches; and in this before us it will be found to be 105711290 English miles.

In order to convey a more just and clear idea of our hydrographic mode of travelling, or how to account for the ship's velocity or speed through the water, it is adjusted or determined by the use of a log, which is either a piece of wood shaped somewhat like the floor part of a boat's bottom, on the keel of which is fixed lead enough to make it swim with that side downward; or else it is in the form of a quarter of a circle, having the circular side loaded with lead enough to make it swim with the angular point upward: In this log is fixed a piece of line, which has a peg at the other end, to fix into a hole in the opposite extremity of the circular side, by means of which the log holds its position in the water; and in the middle or bight of the said piece of line, is bent or made fast another line about 150 fathoms in length: Then 10, 12, or 15 fathoms from the log, is a piece of red rag put thro' the strands, for a mark to turn the glass by; (the space so left is called stray-line, and proportioned to the height of the ship above the water's edge) from that is measured certain equal spaces or lengths on the log-line, which bear the same proportion to a marine mile as half a minute does to an hour. At the first of these divisions, a bit of twine is fastened through the strands of the line, and a knot made on it; at the next division, 2 knots; and so on to 8 or 10; and from these we account the ship's rate of going by so many knots, which mean so many miles an hour. The length of a knot is in proportion as 3600 seconds (the number in an hour) to 6116 feet (the number in a nautical mile) so is 30 seconds to 51 feet nearly; though some mark their line in proportion, so as to have their knot only 7 or $7\frac{1}{2}$ fathoms, and their glass 25 or 26 seconds, making allowance for the difference. However, to prevent a ship being a-head of the reckoning, it is best to use a line marked at about 50 feet to a knot, and use a glass of 28 seconds, instead of half a minute, as some time is necessary for turning the glass and stopping the line; but in a fast sailing ship, when it blows hard, or the vessel is under a press of sail, a quarter-minute glass, or one of only 14 seconds is used, to prevent the trouble of hauling in a great length of line; and in that case, the quantity run out is allowed double, to answer the proportion of half a minute. The log is hove in the following manner – The line being wound on a reel made for that purpose, a man holds it up at the extent of his arms, while the mate or some other person taking and coiling part of the stray-line in his hand, throws the log over the lee quarter clear of the ship's wake, and when the red rag passes through his hands, he cries turn, to another who stands ready with the glass; to which he again cries done; and when he perceives the last particles of sand running out, he says stop: Then stopping the line, he gives a jerk to unfix the peg, and hauls in till he comes at the knots; and after counting, measures how many fathoms he has hauled in; then giving it to another to haul in for reeling up, he marks the rate of her going on the log-board. This experiment is used every hour, in men of war, East Indiamen, and other vessels going on long voyages, where great exactness is required; but in small vessels bound on short voyages, it is done but once in two hours, and the length of line run out doubled, to make it answer to the time. In all these experiments, allowance must be made, from judgement, respecting the way she may have had, more or less, during the hour or two hours; for great variation may be made by the wind veering and hauling, or by its being a steady breeze or squally weather in the time, or the ship's going large sometimes and close hauled at others; also for the send of the sea, &c. The log-board is two smooth pieces of wainscot board joined together with two hinges, with which it shuts to like a book cover that has no leaves in it, and marked with white or yellow lines, dividing it into columns, to contain notes of time, velocity, course, winds, and occurrences, with remarkable transactions done on board, &c. Every time the log is hove, the ship's way is marked throughout the 24 hours, beginning the day at noon; the time between that and midnight is marked P. M. for post meridian; and from midnight to noon the next day, A. M. for ante meridian; also the several shifts of wind and the variations of the ship's course, together with every occurrence worthy notice, is minuted down with chalk; such as reefing top-sails, seeing a sail, tacking or wearing ship, making sail, giving chase, speaking a ship, coming to action, discovering land, &c. &c. And every day, after an observation has been obtained at noon, the several courses are taken off the board upon a slate, and wrought by trigonometrical and other rules of navigation, to find how many miles she has gained in each direction, determine the place she is in, and the bearings and distance of the place sailed from: and also the bearings and distance of the port bound to; or the bearings and distance of any headland from which departure has been taken, or by which a reckoning has been corrected: And ships on a cruise must attend to the bearing and distance of several places in order to their own safety, and their effective operations against an enemy; as they cannot esteem themselves safe unless they can ascertain where they are; and every day's work, when wrought, must be entered in each artist's journal respectively.

The log-book is ruled and marked exactly in the the same manner as the log-board, that past occurrences may be attended to as occasion may require.

FORM of a LOG-BOARD.

H	K	F	Course.	Winds.	Occurrences.
1	6	5	W S W	S	Squally.
2	6	4	W S W $\frac{1}{2}$ W	S $\frac{1}{2}$ W	———
3	6	6	W by S	S by W	———
4	5	1	W	S S W	Saw land.
5	5	2	W	S S W	———
6	5	3	W $\frac{1}{2}$ S	S by W $\frac{1}{2}$ W	———
7	5	6	W by S	S by W	More wind.
8	6	0	W S W	S	———
9	6	2	S W by W	S by E	———
10	6	4	S W	S S E	Saw a sail.
11	6	2	S W	S S E	———
12	6	1	S W by S	S E by S	———
1	6	3	S W by S	S E by S	Gave chase.
2	6	5	S W $\frac{1}{2}$ S	S S E $\frac{1}{2}$ E	———
3	6	5	S S W	S E	———
4	6	6	S S W	S E	———
5	7	2	S S W	S E	———
6	7	4	S by W	S E by E	Fired a gun.
7	7	5	S by W	S E by E	———
8	8	3	W by N	S E by E $\frac{3}{4}$ E	———
9	9	0	W by N	S E by E	———
10	9	3	W by N	S E by E	———
11	9	5	W by N	S E by E	Came to action.
12	2	2	S W by W	S S E	———

Note – H. K. F. signify Hours, Knots, and Fathoms.

11 deg. 15 min. make 1 point of the compass.

22–30–2 points.

33–45–3 points.

45–00–4 points, or a semiquadrant.

90–00–8 points, or a quadrant.

180–00–16 points, or a semicircle.

360–00–32 points, or a great circle.

A Brief Description of Several Countries

I now come to what I proposed, as the supplement of what I have been treating of, viz. to give a further account of several countries situate between the parallels of 60 degrees of north latitude and 40 degrees of south latitude; and between 107 deg. 57 min. of east longitude and 90 degrees of west longitude, which have fallen within the compass of my travels. In this I shall endeavour both to instruct and entertain my readers; in particular, such of them as have not had an opportunity of travelling out of their native country, nor of being otherwise acquainted with the various productions of nature and art.

Having put my manuscript into the hands of a person to correct and prepare for the press, who being a stranger to many of our nautical terms, has changed some of them, especially in the fore end of the narrative, and has also left out several occurrences at sea which probably might be entertaining to divers of my readers, and which I would yet take notice of, but find the limits of my book will not allow it.

Narva being situate in the province of Ingria, commands an extensive trade, which would be much more considerable, was it not for the difficulty of the navigation, which is much impeded by a bar at the mouth of the river, on which there is not more than about 8 or 10 feet of water, which subjects large ships to the disagreeable necessity of riding in an open and dangerous road to take in their loading; and the shores present the melancholy spectacle of the wrecks of ships and vessels warped up in the sand, which is a discouraging sight for a young adventurer to behold. Our vessel, which was only 120 tons burden, was obliged to complete her cargo in the road: The situation made it necessary to work even on Sundays, if the lighters came along side; and the day being more than 18 hours between sunrise and sunset, we got but little rest. This town is regularly built, having several good streets, but many of the houses are constructed of wood, and covered with shingles, i.e. small pieces of thin board clinched to the spars, after the form that flat tiles are laid. It is well fortified and garrisoned with a considerable force; the soldiers are trained up to the use of arms from their childhood, being taken into imperial pay and service at 7 years old, when they have no more than 3 denuscas per day, which are about 3 farthings; the common soldiers' pay is 2 copecks, or 2½d. they are robust and hardy veterans, whose constitutions seem designed to endure hardship and fatigue. The fort always fired a gun morning and evening, while the sun was in the horizon. The Russians in general appear to be a hardy race of people, but working at very low wages, many of them are very indigent, and the want of accommodations makes them slovenly. They are also very much addicted to thieving, so that we were obliged to haul our running-ropes into the tops at night, while we lay at the quay, to prevent them being cut away. They likewise seem inclined to lewdness and ill manners; but their women are exceeding neat and very fair, industrious, and careful: I have seen some of them wade into the river past their knees, and stand there to wash clothes, by beating them on a large stone with a battledoor for many hours together. Some of the Russian laws are severe, and rigorously enforced. A few days after we sailed from hence, we were taken with a gale of wind at W. N. W. which obliged us to lay to under a reefed main course; and it lasting several days, drove us very near a number of little rocks, which are only distinguishable by small flags that are displayed on stages fixed to moorings on them; they lie between Revel and Derwinda: On getting sight of one of these, we wore ship, and laid her head to the northward, by which means we weathered them; and the wind abating and veering round more in our favour, we let the reef out of our main-sail, and set our close-reefed top-sails, which enabled us to lay our course; but our provisions were fallen short, To that the master thought he should be obliged to put us on a stinted allowance; however coming under the island of Burnholm, we hailed a fishing-boat, which coming along side, our master purchased a quantity of herrings. The next day passing thro' Copenhagen road, we obtained a perspective view of his Danish Majesty's beautiful palace and the royal city, and in the evening came to anchor again in Elsinore road, where we procured a supply of bees, rusk, and water. This town is large and handsome, being situate on the south side the Sound, the channel of which lies so near the castle as to be entirely under the command of its guns. No vessel is allowed to pass or repass this place without bringing to, and either paying, or giving security for payment, of the duty demanded by the King of Denmark; and should any ship run pass the castle, there is a frigate always riding in the road ready to slip and go in chase of her. It is about 7 miles across the Sound to Elsimburg on the Swedish shore, and has at times been so hard frozen, as to admit the transporting of heavy artillery over the ice, when the two nations have been at hostility. The adjacent country is sandy and low, interspersed with woods and lawns, and the people are a neat, clean, and industrious race, mostly fair complexioned, with either red or fair hair.

After getting our wants supplied, we put to sea again, but had scarce cleared the land when another gale sprung up at S. S. W. blowing very hard, and the ship being flax loaded, was so crank that she could not bear much canvass when upon a wind; so having Norway under our lee, we put into a Sound called Ripperwick, where we lay till we got a fair wind. In this place we found a Hull Pink, commanded by Mr Thomas Bride, and several other vessels; and our Master differing with Mr Thomas Pentiner, the Mate, he took a note for his wages, and leaving us, shipped in a brig bound for London, and our Master put his son Charles in as Acting Mate. This country is very mountainous, most of it steril, and some quite barren; yet in cavities on the sides of the mountains grow large fir and pine-trees in abundance, together with birch and other small wood. Their staple commodities are timber, raff, tar, turpentine, and fish, with which their coast abounds, especially lobsters and cod, the latter of which they cure without salt in the winter season, by exposing it in the wind and frost, by which they dry up the mois-ture till it becomes as hard as an Egyptian mummy; so that it must be well beaten before it can be boiled: This they call stock-fish, and export great quantities to England and elsewhere, for the use of seamen in long voyages: If kept dry, it will keep sound and good for the space of 20 years or more. The Norse are a hardy and active people; and as many of them who live along the shores are much employed in fishing, they are good pilots for the coast, which abounds with harbours, sounds, and places of shelter. Amongst these pilots are many women well experienced in their profession, who will come off in their boats with their husbands: One of these stepping on board of a vessel, will conduct her safe into a port, while the man is left to manage his boat by himself. These women have so much sagacity, and such knowledge of natural causes and effects, that some have been superstitious enough to give them the appellation of Norway witches. The little vallies contained among or between the hills are very fruitful, being sheltered from the winds, and fructified by the soil washing down from the mountains. Here they raise what corn and vegetables they have room for, but some little is kept for pasturage. We bought a live sheep here for a shilling. The Norse mile is equal to 4 English miles, and the nature of the country forbids travelling many miles a day. Norway is subject to the king of Denmark, but the language here spoken is not pure Danish, but a compound of that and the ancient Norse tongue.

Gotheborg, or Gottenburg, is the second sea-port in the kingdom of Sweden; and in point of commerce, the first: It lies on the western shore not far from the entrance into the Sound, whence the Swedish East Indiamen and most of their West India and other foreign traders are fitted out, and whither they return. It is large and well built, though some of the houses are constructed of wood. The country is mountainous, and many of the hills are almost inaccessible, being high barren rocks; yet they, as well as those of Norway, yield fir and pine timber, which of course produce plenty of rosin, turpentine, tar, and pitch, for exportation: But the Swedes always want a supply of corn from Poland and other countries. The natives are strong, hardy, laborious, civil, ingenious, and of good complexions, and not very careful for fine clothes so they can but procure warm ones: The women wear no stays, or but very few of them; neither do they wear gowns, but jackets and skirts after the manner of the Danes and Dutch women. The current coin of Sweden is chiefly silver and copper; the latter being very abundant in that country, they make large plates of it, which being stamped in the middle and at the four corners, each passes for its value, which they reckon by dollars silver marc and dollars copper marc; and small sums are reckoned by stivers, as we count by pence. The coast and harbour abounding, at the time I was there, with herrings, the streets of the city near the quays were filled with barrels of fish, and every ship in the harbour had her quarters hung round with herrings: Our Master bought so many for our use, that we subsisted on them till we were fully convinced that salt beef suited our palates better. On leaving this port, we had not proceeded far past the beakon, known by the name of wingo beakon, when we were suddenly taken a-back by a strong gale at W. by N. and

thereby obliged to put back into Stral Sound, where we found the
Snow *Hamburg* merchant of Hull, and sailed thence in company
with her 3 days after; and when having got within sight of the
Naze, a gale sprung up at S. W. by W. and obliged each vessel to
bring to under a balanced trey-sail, she laying her head to the
southward, and we with our head to the northward, which caused
a separation, and occasioned very different land falls; she, by falling
into the southward of the spurn, gained her port; but the gale continuing for 8 days, we drifted much out of our way. After we had
lashed our helm a-lee, we fixed some deals in our weather main
shrouds, as a weather-board, to break the force of the sea; and
divided ourselves into 4 two-hour watches, we being 8 in number.
The sea running mountains high, she would often ship whole seas,
and wash away every loose thing off the deck; and one night while
Mr Thomas Lundie, the Mate, and I were on the watch from 12 to
2 A. M. as I stood at the binacle to observe how she fell off and came
to, she, by falling off about 4 points, and labouring in the trough of
the sea, shipped such a weight of water as drove me from my station, and so immersed me, that I only knew by the sensation of my
feet whether I was within-board or without. On the gale abating,
we made sail; and after some days made the land, which proved to
be Coquet island on the coast of Northumberland, and afterward
put into Tynemouth haven, where we stopped only two tides before
the wind coming in our favour, we sailed, and arrived at home just
a week after our consort.

Outward-bound to Havre in January, 1755, we were forced to
bring up in Yarmouth roads, where we rode out a hard gale of
wind which began at S. E. then veered round to E. N. E. and blew
so hard that our anchor came home, and obliged us to let go the
best-bower and strike our yards and topmasts, and with pointing
our yards to the wind, she rode it out, rolling so at her anchor
(owing to the nature of her loading) that she shipped water over
one gunwale and threw it over the other. Many vessels broke from
their anchors and ran for Harwich, where they might run a-ground
on the mud and be safe if they had neither anchor nor cable. A lute-
sterned Snow, belonging to Boston in New England, went ashore
among the ice and snow on the beach, where she was lost.

Havre-de-Grace is the principal sea-port in the province of
Normandy, though not so large a place as Rouen, which is the

capital; it is well fortified, and the mole or bason is commodious
enough to contain 300 sail of ships and vessels; but the harbour,
exclusive of the said dock, is not very eligible, on account of the
rapidity of the tide, which is supposed to run near 20 knots on the
flood at the spring tides, which is occasioned by the form of the
adjacent shores; so that vessels lying high and dry on the mud will
be floated in a little time, when the tide begins to rush into the
haven, where they are as suddenly deserted on the tide of ebb. The
buildings are neat and elegant, and the city is formed on a beautiful
plan. The market is well supplied and numerously attended. The
manners of the French nation are so well known in Great Britain,
that I need say but little about them; as very few need to be told that
the inhabitants of that country are inclined to foppery: Some of the
gentlewomen wear stays and fine shoes, &c. while the poor, and
especially the country girls, wear neither stays nor shoes, except
such as are made of wood, which are pieces of willow hollowed out
in the form of a clumsy shoe, and lined with bits of lamb-skin, to
prevent it from bruising the foot.

Madeira is well situated in the Atlantic for the convenience of
ships sailing to the East or West Indies, where they can get a supply
of wood and water, and furnish themselves with wines either for
their own consumption or for merchandise. The chief town is
Funchal. This island is subject to Portugal, as are also the other
Canary and western islands, or most of them. Some of the mountains are a stupendous height; I have seen clouds of condensed air
and vapor lodge in cavities far beneath their summit, which
appeared conspicuously above them. The air is salubrious, and the
climate very mild; which, joined to some other local circumstances,
render it delightful.

Something of Barbadoes has been already mentioned; I shall
further observe, that for the extent of it, it is not to be exceeded
either for beauty or fruitfulness, yielding rich canes which produce
great quantities of sugar, rum, and molasses; also cotton, indigo,
cochineal, cocoa, and cocoa nuts; likewise bananas, plantains,
guavases, mangas, &c. The inhabitants are composed of English,
Scotch, Irish, Creoles, Mustees, Mulattas, and Negroes; the latter of
which, though they are chiefly slaves, are by far the most in
number. Some of these denominations may require a little explanation to make them intelligible – A Creole is a white person born on

the island; the Mustees are such as have one white and one mulatta parent; Mulattas are such as have one white and one black parent; and Negroes are such as are entire black, with a sort of short curly hair like wool: Such blacks as have long flank hair are not called Negroes. All blacks are white when born, but presently change their colour. Many of these are imported from Africa; which country being held by different Princes and Chiefs, they go to war with each other; and if in an engagement between these contending powers, any prisoners are taken unhurt, they are sold to Europeans trading down the coast; and sometimes parents sell their children, and others their nearest relations. These unhappy creatures are bartered for on the coast of Guinea, at the rate of about 5 or 6l. a head, on an average, and carried to the West Indies and America, where they are exposed to sale on board a guineaman as naked as our first parents in Paradise, save only a hippen made of red cloth given to the women to serve in the place of a fig-leaf covering, when the planters go and buy them, as our people in England go to a fair to buy cattle, and give from 50 to 60l. a piece for full-grown slaves. With respect to dress, it is various; some of the white men wear light thin suits from head to foot, and some do not. Some of the white women too wear full light suits, except stays; whereas some wear neither stays, hat, nor shoes. Some of the women of colour wear only a sconce to hide their nakedness; and some men, particularly the negroes, go as naked as they were born. The women slaves desire to be pregnant for more reasons than many of our free-born Englishwomen do, as it procures them milder treatment, and some relaxation from their labour. I have often wondered how their pickininies, i.e. children ever learned to run, as they are frequently left to sprawl about on the sand in or at the doors of the wigwams while the mothers are at work. Some of these people are of as bright a genius as those that rule over them: They suppose they are to return to their native country when they die, and from such a delusion they rejoice at the funerals of their deceased friends, dancing, singing, and playing on such musical instruments as they have, such as the tomtom, i.e. a sort of drum, &c. and using other expressions of joy. This beautiful island was the first in the West Indies that was colonized by the English: It was almost destroyed in October, 1780, by a most dreadful hurricane or storm of wind, rain, thunder, and lightening, which carried all before it, viz. trees, houses, mills, &c. many lost their lives, and many more the support of life: For the relief of such, the British parliament voted 80000l. The chief town is Bridge-Town, which was entirely demolished by the afore mentioned catastrophe. Spikeses is also a pretty town, but not favoured with a good bay like the former. The sun is to the northward of this isle 3 months and 24 days, and southward 8 months and 6 days, in the year.

Antigua is 20 miles long and 20 broad, and produces great quantities of sugar, rum, molasses, cotton, indigo, &c. also a great variety of tropical fruits, such as those before mentioned; and also papa-apples, mama-apples, prickly pears, alligator pears, soursops, &c. Here is likewise a fruit called a mangineal apple, which is beautiful to behold, but so corrosive in its nature, that one of them would do as much mischief as an ounce of arsenic; and the bushes on which they grow are of such a quality, that water dropping from the leaves will raise blisters. This and every one of the Caribbee islands also yield plenty of tamarinds, which grow on large trees in long pods somewhat resembling those of a windsor bean. Here is also variety of roots and vegetables, such as yams, sweet potatoes, pompions, water-melons, musk-melons, ockery, and calalu: Also spice, such as cod-pepper, cayan pepper, &c. Fresh provisions are always scarce and dear, as there is but little pasturage; and water is an article of such value, that one might sometimes almost as easily obtain a drink of rum. Columbus, who first discovered this island, on finding no water, soon abandoned it again, and gave it the name of Anti-Augo, which signifies no water, or an enemy to water; nevertheless it is of great consequence now to England. The planters and others are obliged to catch rain water in tanks or cisterns, which are made as follows, viz, they dig a square trench like a cellar, which they pave at the bottom, wall at the sides, and arch over at the top; then inclose a compass round it with a wall, and pave the ground so taken in (above the tank) with a descent, inclining to a gullyhole, where it runs down, and whence it may be drawn out again with a bucket. These will hold and preserve a great deal of water. They have them now in plenty in several parts: There is one of large dimension on Monk's hill, for the garrison, and another at English Harbour, for the navy. When this expedient fails, as in a dry season, the islanders are oft obliged to fetch water in boats from Montserrat, which is at the distance of 12 leagues; and king's ships,

&c. are forced to go thither, or to St Kit's, to water for a cruise, though a small supply of good water may be obtained at Cade's bay, where they have a well made, by a cask without a bottom being sunk in the ground. The inhabitants, and their manners and customs, are much the same as at Barbadoes, to which I refer my readers, and also for the rest of these islands. St John's is the capital of this island, which is well fortified by batteries on Rat-island, in the entrance of the harbour, which is safe and commodious; and below the said isle, there is a fine large bay, called St John's road, where a large fleet may ride at safe anchorage. In this bay there is abundance of excellent fish, such as gore-fish, cavallies, snappers, old-wives, &c. and some dolphins and sharks. We caught one of the latter here 11 feet long, and used it as extra provision. There are some other bays on the north side of the island, but none of consequence. English Harbour is a very safe place for ships, being encircled with very high land, except at the entrance. Here is a very good yard, with every thing necessary for heaving down such of His Majesty's ships as are in want of cleaning or slight repair: Also an arsenal and magazine; the harbour being admissible to ships of the line, which must take care to keep the north shore aboard as they come in, where the water is so clear that I have seen fishes amongst the weeds as intelligible as though there had been no more than 3 feet depth of water. As this was the place of our general rendezvous, I have some particulars to relate. In the beginning of 1757, while we were preparing to heave down, being about to carry an anchor ashore on a catamaran, which was scarce sufficient to bear the weight of it, I, and two more who were not much acquainted with the art of swimming, got into the long-boat, fearing what might ensure; yet not observing that the boat's painter was fast to the ring of the anchor, it proved to be an unsafe asylum; for no sooner were the tackles unhooked, than the stage careened and let the anchor slide off, which instantly drew the boat down after it, and set us all afloat. I at first caught hold of a man, but knowing he could not swim, I let him go to shift for himself, and next seized an oar, but had it pulled from me by another who wanted it for the same purpose I did: This obliged me to try how I could swim, which I performed (sometimes above and at others under the water) till I got hold of the fore-yard tackle; and by nipping the fall, got astride on the block, from whence I looked round to see what was become of the rest. There I remained till a boat came and took me off, so a belly-full of salt water was the greatest inconvenience I sustained from the accident. While preparing to heave down, our prize-money for the Pacific being still in the Agent's hands at St John's and we in want of it, a plot was contrived by some of us to go thither, and by forcible means procure payment: Accordingly 31 of us rushed out of the yard at 2 o'clock, when the hands were called to work, and forcing past the Sentinel he fired three shots, but without effect, any more than giving the alarm. Having a steep hill to ascend, many passed by me as I ran, being only just recovered from sickness: This rather brought a damp on my spirits, supposing I should be taken first, and in consequence thereof the Lieutenant (the Captain being a prisoner) would punish me before the rest came back. However, making a halt on the top of the hill, it was there unanimously agreed, not to separate nor abandon each other, whatever might be the result. We then marched forward, supposing we should soon be pursued by the soldiers from one of the forts, but were impeded by a party of the island militia, who stopped us at Falmouth about the space of two hours, the whole island being under an alarm at the appearance of a fleet to windward; but as soon as it was known to be English, we, on having told our errand, were suffered to proceed, and accordingly took our route about 5 o'clock, after having sent one of our party back as unable to perform the journey. The unusual appearance of so many men passing on the road, excited astonishment in the Negroes in the plantations bordering on it, who left their work, and said to each other as we passed them, Kie buccara man. When we came on St John's green, we put to flight a number of privateer's men who were playing at cricket, they taking us for a press-gang, as we came in a body; but as we had no officer with us, they at last made a halt for us to come up, and gave us what punch they had amongst us, and sent a Negro boy to shew us where to find Admiral Frankland, whose advice we wanted, and forgiveness too, as we had come without leave, both which we obtained; and being asked what we intended to do with the Agent, we told him we would pull his house down if he would give us leave; but he advised us not to offer any violence, but choose two men from amongst us who should go and tell Colonel Lafley, from him, that he insisted on him making us some payment in a few days, as he saw our necessity; there being 27 of us out of 30 bare-foot. Having obtained his word and honour to indemnify us from being punished, we returned back and got to English Harbour about 12 o'clock at night, having travelled 24 miles without any thing to eat; and on going aboard, I found my messmate, who stayed behind, had given all the beef and pudding away to the Negro girls; so I was forced to go to my hammock without any supper. However in a few days we were paid about 6l. sterling, which made some amends; but the remainder, amounting to about 30l. was never paid. While we continued at the wharf, we were presented with a very uncommon sight, viz. a Negro woman having been guilty of some small misdemeanor on board the *Bristol* of 50 guns, they first whipped her, then stript her quite naked, besmeared her with tar from head to foot, sprinkled feathers thereupon, and sent her ashore. – I suppose this female harlequin might have easily gained a conquest over one of our country market towns in England; for had she entered it in the twilight of the evening, they would readily have imagined that old Pluto's consort, Proserpina, had left the infernal plains to pay them a visit. Not long after this, Captain Cummings served a white girl nearly in the same manner, by causing her to be stripped down to her waist, tarred and feathered, rowed ashore, and set on the wharf in the presence of Admiral Frankland and Captains Le Cras, Lisle, &c. This harbour being free from sharks, which infest the open seas and roads, the Negro women having sugar, sugar-canes, fish, greens, yams, potatoes, oranges, plantains, bananas, pine-apples, cashue nuts, scalions, casava bread, prickly pears, &c. to bring on board, they will frequently, in the absence of the boats, put their several commodities together, with what little apparel they wear, into a half tub; then launching it off the shore, they will swim after it, pushing it on before them till they come along side a ship, and receiving help from some of the crew, they get their goods on board; then dry and dress themselves, and stand their market till they have sold their articles: They then again undress, deposit their clothes in the tub, launch it overboard, jump after it, and return ashore, unless one of the ship's boats be at liberty; when in such case, they mostly obtain the shore by a more eligible means of conveyance. Sailing from St John's on a cruise, we saw a brigg, under English colours, in chase of a sloop, which shewed no colours; and tacking, stood for them, and fired at the brigg, and she fired at the chase several times, till at

length we gave over the pursuit, but the brigg continued here till
the sloop had arrived under the protection of Rat-island sort, and
hoisted English colours; and the brigg hoisting French colours,
fired at her, and hauled to the southward of the island, while we
were beating up on the north side, and thus made her escape.

Having said something already about the populous and splendid city of New York, I shall only observe further, that its situation
gives it the greatest advantages both for inland navigation and foreign trade, which renders it an emporium of commerce, and causes
a large confluence of people of every description to reside there; so
that the inhabitants are a composition of almost every nation of
Europe and the different parts of the American continent, with
many of several Indian tribes, and such as have been imported from
Africa; each of which retain something of the principles in which
they have been instructed in their youth, which cause great variety
in both habit and sentiment. The sun is on their meridian when he
is 4 hours, 59 minutes, and 24 seconds below the meridian of
London; so that when they sit down to dinner, the people in
England begin to enquire what the Cook is preparing for supper, it
being almost 5 o'clock at London when it is noon at New York.

Montserrat is a small island, part of which is mountainous, and
the other part very fertile, producing sugar-canes, &c. and even the
mountains produce wood and various kinds of tropical fruits and
vegetables. The air is good, and there is a tolerable good bay on the
S. W. side of the island, where there is very good water, but not very
easy to be got off, by reason of the surf which runs very high at
times. Amongst the Europeans, either settled or resident here, there
are so many Irish, that it has been sometimes called Little Ireland;
and some of the old Caribbs and Negroes can speak the language. It
lies S. W. ¾ S. from Antigua, and nearly W. by N. from Guadaloupe.

A few leagues N. W. of Montserrat, lies a remarkable rock,
called Rodonda, which takes its name from a flying fish, as it
resembles one of them very much in a view from the N. E. This
pyramid is almost inaccessible on every side, yet it appears somewhat level at the top, and very verdant, but has not so much as a
tree or bush upon it, nor any animal except a few goats. Off this
island, as we were going to Old Road for water in July, 1756, we
espied a large ship to leeward of us, which having lost her main
mast, was going right before the wind; we gave chase to her for

some time, until the wind died away and veered to the southward, so that it became necessary to make a trip; when, the ship missing stays for want of wind, the Master ordered the sweeps out at the gun-room ports to bring her round; but Captain Watkins perceiving it, ordered us to launch them in again, fearing lest she should be a line of battle ship, and we should be becalmed under the command of her guns, and so obliged to surrender to superior force. Thus we missed a favourable opportunity of making our fortunes; she being, as we afterwards learned, a French East Indiaman bearing away for Cape Francois, where she arrived and laid 11 months refitting and waiting for convoy to Europe.

Nevis is a small island that lies so contiguous to St Kit's, that they appear as one when viewed from St John's in Antigua: It is low and fruitful, except some hills in the centre and towards the N. W. shore, which are of considerable height. The bay is safe and commodious, and the water is good and plentiful. In July, 1757, the trade being assembled at St John's, the Admiral sailed with his whole force to escort it past Anguilla and Sambarrera, to about 20 degrees of north latitude, when the *Antigua* sloop of 16 guns carrying away her mast by the swaying of the boom, the Admiral made the signal for us to take her in tow, which caused our separation from the fleet; and some days after that, we put in here for wood and water. The night after we left the bay, two Antigua privateers came up to us, and, without hailing, fired their broad-sides at us: We soon returned the favour very warmly, until they sheered off (seeming to be satisfied with what they had got) without having done us any considerable damage; but in our hurry, we had cast off the tow; and while both we and the sloop were engaged, she dropped astern of the privateers and we lost sight of her; and not knowing but they were French, we supposed they had taken her, which drove Captain Cummings almost to distraction; as it would have reflected much disgrace on his conduct, and exposed him to a court martial: However we saw and gave chase to a sail next day, which proved to be one of them; and bringing her to, sent our boat on board, with a Lieutenant, who reprimanded the Captain for his behaviour; but he hailed us, and told our Captain to order his Lieutenant on board again or he would throw him overboard, saying, his commission was as good as his; and being conscious of his diminutive force, he was justifiable in taking all advantages.

However we saw no more of the *Antigua* till we saw her in English Harbour with two masts, being rigged into a brigg. Nevis, when viewed in one direction, resembles a ship under her courses and top-sails, and from thence derives its name. It is under the orders of the Governor of St Kit's.

St Kit's, or St Christopher's, derives its name from Christopher Columbus, its first discoverer: It lies 18 leagues W. by N. from Antigua. Though the interior parts are mountainous, and yield but little except wood and some fruits, yet the vallies and plains, which lie towards the shores, are exceedingly fertile, and produce a proportionate quantity of sugar, rum, coffee, cotton, &c. The chief town is called Basseterre, or best land; it affords one of the most beautiful perspective views I have ever seen, when beheld from a convenient offing at sea, it being surrounded with cocoa-nut trees and tamarind-trees, &c. which (as in all countries within the torrid zone) have a perpetual verdure. The trees do indeed cast their leaves, but they are never destitute; for while some are falling off, others are shooting forth: Add to this the various cotton plantations and sugar-cane plats, interspersed with wind mills, &c. all which render it delightful. As sugar is the chief product of all the American islands, known by the name of the West Indies, it may not be disagreeable to some readers to have a particular account of it, and how it is brought to perfection. It grows somewhat in the form of wheat when in the blade, but much larger; the canes, when full grown, being many of them 4, 5, or 6 inches in circumference; and from 5 to 7 or 8 feet in height. When it is fit for cutting, they do not reap it down and gather it into barns as we do the produce of our lands in England, but cut it and immediately take it to the mill, which is always made to go with the wind, and is constructed with one main post, which runs perpendicular from top to bottom, and turns upon its heel: This post is shod or cogged with iron, about $2\frac{1}{2}$ or 3 feet in length, and has two side posts cogged in like manner, on either side one, which are placed so near the main post as to lock into its cogs on either side, and be turned round by it. Between these cogs the small ends of the canes are entered by the Negroes, so that the mill draws them through, and squeezes all the juice out into a cistern, whence it is conveyed by a spout into a furnace, and runs from that into another, where it boils to the consistence of what we term raw sugar. It is then put into a vessel which has its bottom full of holes, with a reserver underneath it, into which the molasses drain; part of which is put into casks for exportation, and the residue is distilled into rum. The manner in which the Negroes catch monkies in the mountains here, may afford amusement to some: They take a cocoa-nut and make a hole in the end large enough for the monkey to put in his paw; then loosen a quantity of the nut in the shell, and lay it in a track where the monkies frequent; and when one of them comes, he will put in his fist and grasp so much that he cannot pull it out again; so that he is shackled with the cocoa-nut, and will suffer himself to be taken before he'll quit his hold. Basseterre Bay is very large and commodious, and being well sheltered by the S. E. point of Nevis, is a very good and safe road for a great number of ships, except in the hurricane months, when the wind veers round to other points of the compass, and then no place in the West Indies can be deemed perfectly safe; for which reason it is always thought advisable to leave the islands before the hurricane season sets in. To the westward of the promontory which bounds the leeward extremity of this bay, there is an excellent watering place called Old Road, but the surf running so high, renders it so difficult of access, that the long-boats are obliged to lie off at grapnels; and when the waterers have filled their gang-casks, they are forced to swim them off by pushing them before 'em to the boats, where they either hoist or parbuckle them in. There is also a pretty good watering-place at Sandy Point on the west end of the island, from whence the inhabitants of the neighbouring island of St Eustatia get a supply of that necessary article, having very little of their own. This island and Montserrat afford the best water of any of the Leeward islands for keeping at sea or otherwise. The currency here, and at Antigua, Montserrat, Nevis, and Tortola, is 50 per cent. beneath sterling; and at Barbadoes and Jamaica, 25 per cent. beneath it; so that there, 1s. passes for 15d. and here for 18d. or 18 dogs. This isle is fortified wherever it is accessible, but the principal place of strength is Brimstone Hill. One dark night, having got near one of the forts, they fired at us; and not being able to make them understand by our signals what we were, they continued to annoy and alarm us for some time, till by stretching off shore we were out of their reach, without receiving any other damage than the carrying away of our main top-mast spring-stay and some running-rigging.

Carthagena is situate in South America, although it lies in north
latitude; for the two continents, or rather peninsulas, are connected
together, and the boundary of each is fixed by the isthmus of
Darien, between Porto-Bello on the N. E. and Panama on the S. W.
It is the principal place in the Spanish settlements on that part of
the main called Golden Castile, which borders on the Caribbean
sea, and is built at the upper extremity of a commodious harbour,
into which the entrance is very narrow, and fortified on the larboard side by Bucha Chica castle, and on the starboard side by St
Joseph's fort; both which are of prodigious strength, but were
reduced by Admiral Vernon in 1740, which gave him admission
into the harbour, yet he was not successful in his enterprize against
the town. It is healthful to such as have acquired a habit of bearing
heat, having a good air and dry seasons. The adjacent country is
varigated with hills and vallies; and on an eminence at some distance from the city, there is a large nunnery, called Mother-o-poop,
whither the opulent amongst the besieged removed their treasure
during the fore-mentioned siege, it being deemed impregnable
from the fortifications that were erected on that occasion. The coast
abounds with excellent tortoise; and as these are creatures but little
known to some people in England, I shall therefore give some
description of them. They are of four sorts, one of which, as it
always abides on shore, is called the land-tortoise: The other three
are denominated as follows, viz. the hawk's-bill, green, and logger-
head-tortoise; the latter of which is very gross, and if subsisted on
long together, would cause blotches and cutaneous eruptions; but
the hawk's-bill and green tortoise are very delicious food; the fat of
the latter is like marrow, but green as grass, from whence it derives
its name. They are inclosed in very herculian shells, except the
head, neck, and some of the hinder parts, with the fins, which are
but slightly guarded against harms. The head resembles that of a
parrot; the neck, that of a lamb; and the fins (which are four in
number) are like a hand without a thumb and the fingers webbed
together, having strong and pointed nails: With these they walk
when on shore, and swim when in the water; for being amphibious,
they can live either on land or in water, as they please: When they
are turned on their backs, especially ashore, no creature is so help-
less, as they cannot by any means whatever recover themselves; and
when taken, frequently subsist many days on a ship's deck without

receiving any other refreshment than the washing their eyes with clean salt water, and will mourn and shed tears. They submit to the knife as a sheep does. The shell may be disjointed with a knife: The back shell consists of 13 pieces of various and beautiful colours, and the belly shell is a fine straw-coloured yellow. They are said to be fish, flesh, and fowl; the first, from their going in the water and subsisting on sea weeds; the second, from their coming on the land and eating grass; and the latter, from their females laying eggs (though they are without shells, having only strong rinds) which they cover with sand and leave them to batch by the warmth of Sol's prolific beams; forgetting that a foot might accidentally crush them. These amphibians, when small, are called chickens; but when full grown, they weight from 5 to 7 cwt. apiece; and their shells are so strong, that they would bear a great weight without hurting them. Fourteen of these and two bullocks were given us at each time of our being here. Parrots are very numerous here, particularly those of the green colour, commonly called main-birds: They fly about in covies as pigeons do in England, and with as little molestation. Here is also some grey birds which talk as well or better than the green ones, but not like the African parrots. The inhabitants consist chiefly of European-Spaniards, Creoles, and Indians; the whole computed to about 40000 souls. When we first came to anchor in Bucha Chica road, a Portuguese youth, who had begged a passage of Captain Cummings while we lay at Greenwich in Jamaica, presented himself on the gangway when the boat was manned to go ashore; and being restrained by the Sentinel, he turned to the Captain and began to exclaim, O Signior Captine, me star passengier, me vamus etterra, me star passengier; but was answered, get along, you rascal; and on his insisting that he was only a passenger, the Captain ordered him to be put into the bilboes and kept a prisoner during our stay and also at our return, but was let out to work in the day-time, it being understood that he had eloped from his Master at Philadelphia, and so was deemed a fit person to serve His Majesty. While we continued here, two Spanish guardacostas (a frigate and a xebeck) sailed past us, bound on a cruise in the bays of Honduras and Campeachy.

Porto-Bello, or Port Desire, though but a little detached from Carthagena, is very different with respect to air and weather; for the atmosphere being always impregnated with humidity along this coast, the rains are almost perpetual, which cause the rich soil to produce abundance of spontaneous fruits and vegetables, the greatest part of which perish on the ground for want of gathering; as the inhabitants consist of little more than a garrison supported by government, and consequently don't wish to work; and the Indians are kept at a distance. – Of what value would these pine-apples, cocoa-nuts, melons, &c. be in some places, which here are suffered to rot and help to manure the ground, which is naturally as prolific as a dung-hill or hot-bed! This place is never troubled with hurricanes, nor can it even be said ever to blow so much as a gale of wind; but the incessant rains, and the exhalations raised from the ground occasioned by an almost vertical sun, generate fevers, fluxes, &c. so that Admiral Hoster, who formed a long blockade in 1738, fell a victim to them, together with a great number of brave seamen, while he was, by his orders, restrained from assailing the place with 20 ships of the line, while matters hung in suspense between the two nations; notwithstanding it surrendered to Vice Admiral Vernon on the 22d of November, 1739, who, in concert with Commodore Brown, had only 6 sail of the line, a 20 gun ship, and a sloop, under their joint command, beside a number of land forces. While we remained here, the garrison was in continual alarm from some of the Indians who had appeared in force in the vicinity of the town, and had also intercepted some of their caravans on the road from Panama, cut off the men, and carried away the mules with their loading. Here are also abundance of parrots; likewise monkies and marmosets, which live upon the spontaneous fruits in the woods. As we were leaving the harbour, the two guarda-costas afore mentioned were coming in there from their cruise, with an English sloop-prize they had taken in the bay of Honduras (she being engaged in the force, or bucaniering trade) some of the poor prisoners hailed us, and bid us farewel! expecting to be conveyed across the isthmus into some part of Peru, 'and, there be plung'd in mines, forget a sun was made!!!' Not that they could so forget; but by being confined in a deep cavern of the earth, and excluded the benefit of the sun's genial rays, or even the least gleam of natural light, the sun was thenceforth for them made in vain. This is the worst kind of slavery – to be consigned to wear out the sad remains of a wretched life in delving for treasure to enrich and ornament others; and when worn out with labour and ill treatment, to be interred amongst the rubbish, and there forgotten!

Jamaica was discovered by Columbus, and in part taken possession of by the Spaniards, and afterwards Hernando Cortes and some other Spanish commanders, who found excuses for extirpating the native Indians, and subduing the whole island to the dominion of the King of Spain; but Admiral Penn and General Venebales, commanding the British forces serving under Oliver Cromwell, took it from the Spaniards in the year 1655. Port Royal was once the capital, but it was almost ruined by an earthquake in 1692, and its remains nearly destroyed by a dreadful fire in 1702, so that the Governor's residence was removed to Spanish-Town; but now Kingston is the capital. Besides these, there are several towns of considerable importance, such as Port Anthony; Savannah-la-mar, &c. and Port Royal, although it has suffered so much, and lost so much ground that large ships now ride at anchor where part of it stood, yet it is flourishing in proportion to the size of it; and, commanding the entrance into Kingston harbour, and being the arsenal for the King's naval stores, together with a good yard and wharf for heaving down ships of any rate, it is still of the greatest national importance. This town, as well as the other West India cities and towns, is in part built of wood and covered with shingles, and many of the houses have no glass windows. The island, which is by far the greatest colony in the West Indies subject to his Britannic Majesty (though much less than the neighbouring islands of Cuba and Hispaniola) is divided into 16 counties, most of which are rich, well planted, and populous: In some parts, indeed, there are mountains of a stupendous height; in particular those in the middle of the island, called the Blue Mountains, from the clouds resting below their summits: But these produce large mahogany and cedar trees, together with some logwood; and the levels are exceeding fruitful, yielding the fattest canes in the world, and consequently their sugar and rum are the best. Besides which, it produces great quantities of cocoa, cochineal, indigo, cotton, coffee, pepper, ginger, pimento, tobacco, &c. great quantities of which are yearly exported to England, Ireland, and America. They also carry on a considerable trade in log-wood brought from the Mosquito shore, which traffic is sometimes carried beyond its limits; it produced the war with

Spain in 1739. Here are also tropical fruits of all kinds, in great
plenty, with variety of vegetables, &c. Here they have many artificial salt-ponds, where the earth being taken away about 12 or 14
inches below the surface of the sea, and parted from it by a small
ridge, through which the water is let in to fill the pond, it is there
congealed by the heat of the sun, and dried to the consistence of salt.
In the mountains, the air is serene and healthful; but in the plains,
and other parts, it is far otherwise; for the sea-breeze generally
dying away in the evening, it falls a flat calm, and in about two
hours after, is succeeded by a land-breeze, which is exceeding sultry, and renders the night less salubrious than the day; for on the
return of the sea-breeze about 10 o'clock in the morning, the brisk
air is so refreshing that the Negroes call it the Doctor. Sometimes
this breeze will continue for 3 or 4 days together, and then it is
termed the fiery sea-breeze, because it blows hard at sea and prevails against the current of land air. This island has repeatedly
suffered great damage by hurricanes, whereby some plantations
have been nearly destroyed, and ships have been carried from their
anchors in Port Royal harbour quite upon the plain on the back of
Greenwich hospital, and left there at the falling of the water when
the storm abated and the flood subsided to its former course. In
October, 1780, the leeward part of the island sustained much
injury by a hurricane, particularly about Savannah-la-mar and
Cumberland County; for the relief of which, the British parliament
voted 40000l. In some of the rivers, and particularly Black river,
there is a great number of alligators, which are nearly in the shape
of a newt or lizard, but are large and voracious, so as to kill and
devour a man in a very little time. They are, when full grown, from
12 to 16 feet long; have 4 short legs, a long tail, a prodigious wide
mouth, very canine teeth, and are all over set with strong scales, so
as to be almost impenetrable by a musket ball: They are amphibious creatures, and can live in either air or water for a time; but if
they catch any prey in the water, they cannot eat it there, because
they have no gills as a fish hath: They are much like a crocodile,
and some say, only differ from it by the movement of their jaws in
taking their food; the crocodile working the upper jaw, and the alligator the lower one. Here is also another creature which greatly
resembles these, called a guana, but much less, and always lives
ashore: They are sometimes eaten by the slaves. Upon the coast, and

in the bays and harbours, there are a great number of sharks: These are a rapacious kind of fishes, and also man-eaters; some of them are 16 or 18 feet long; they have a very keen appetite, but slow at taking their prey; their teeth, of which they have several rows, are very sharp, and resemble those of a whip saw: They are of two kinds, one of which are called white sharks; these always swim on or near the surface of the water; and the other, blue or shovel-nosed sharks, which lie at the bottom, and seldom appear but when some prey presents itself to view. A boat oversetting one day under the *Marlborough*'s stern, one of these sprang up and bit one of the men in two before assistance could be got. And once coming off from Greenwich to Port Royal in the long-boat, with a fresh sea-breeze, I had like to have shared a similar fate; for one of the men having lost his hat, we put the boat about for it; and by reaching to catch it as we passed, I had well nigh launched overboard head-foremost, and proved the truth of what I here assert concerning blue sharks, there being great numbers of them in the harbour. There are many land crabs in the swamps, which will scratch through the earth into the graves of the dead. The inhabitants are composed of Europeans, Creoles, Mustees, Mulattas, and Negroes; but here, as well as in all the other West India islands, the greatest part are people of colour, there being perhaps six of these to one white, including soldiers; yet notwithstanding their superiority in number, they are often ruled with much rigor. The manner of punishing them at the wharfs for crimes beneath the cognizance of the Magistrate, is as follows – They seize a $\frac{1}{2}$ cwt. to each foot, and then lash both hands together, which they likewise fasten to the wheel of a setting crane, by which they are stretched to their full length, so that they cannot shrink from the stroke: They then whip 'em with platted thongs which they call a cow-skin: This is continued during the Master or Superintendant's pleasure; and it is then succeeded by flogging with ebony bushes, which resemble our goose-berry bushes in England, till their skins are filled as full of pricks as a porcupine is of quills; and when these are extracted, the poor wretch is left full of bleeding wounds to emit the blood. I have seen some of them stand at liberty to receive their punishment with such invincible resolution, as not to shrink or stir in the least, degree, though they have been cut to the bone; while others have borne it with quite a different temper and deportment. This island is fortified wherever it is deemed vulnerable; but the greatest attention has been paid to the fortification of Port Royal harbour; and even if the outward works should be carried by an assailing force, there are several strong batteries on the left hand by the salt-ponds; in particular, one almost level with the water's edge, on which is mounted 12 thirty-two pounders, called the 12 Apostles or Special Messengers. The two midsummer days here are the 10th of May and 2d of August; and during the shortest space of time between these periods, which is 85 days, the earth has but a traverse of 11 deg. 38 miles; I mean while the sun's declination exceeds this parallel of latitude; in the middle of which space is the longest day, which is about 13 hours and 46 minutes: And in the longest space of 280 days, she makes a traverse or transit of 82 deg. 18 miles: In the middle of this period, (while the earth is in Cancer and the sun in Capricorn) is their shortest day, which is 10 hours and 14 minutes. When it is 12 o'clock at London, it is only 53 min. and 28 seconds past 6 in the morning here; so that while the inhabitants of Jamaica are getting their breakfasts, those of London are about to sit down to dinner.

Charles-Town is not only the chief town in the province of South Carolina, but the principal place of trade, from whence the produce of the country is exported to England and other places. It is situate on a point at the fall of Ashley river; it stands low, and the adjacent parts are also low flat land, and much of it swampy, so that it produces plentiful crops of rice, which will not grow unless it be watered; hence a dry season, in a rice country, occasions scarcity, and sometimes famine. This is one of the staple commodities of the country; besides which they have of late years raised a great deal of indigo. They also export large quantities of deer-skins, as this province abounds with those creatures, venison is much more plentiful, and of less esteem, than in many other places. They have likewise abundance of horned cattle, sheep, and goats, so that provisions are generally plentiful and very cheap; yet they were wont to make rice supply the place of bread, especially for the servants and slaves. Intense frosts are never known here: some frost indeed they have, but the ice seldom exceeds the thickness of a half-crown piece; neither have they any snow, yet it is unhealthful; for as the land is low and full of fresh water lakes, rivers, and swamps, it makes a change of wind pernicious; as when it blows out of the sea, it is very hot, particularly in summer; but if it suddenly shift and blow off the land, the effect of such change is presently and very sensibly felt; for the cold, in a few minutes, chills the blood, and frequently causes agues, fevers, and fluxes. While the colonists were subject to the avaricious views of our English merchants, every article of cloathing was scarce and dear, and most of the people in Carolina were glad to content themselves with such garments as they could procure, while decoration in dress was out of question. The inhabitants consist of Europeans, descendants from Natives of Europe, Indians, and Negroes, with some who are of the half blood, or Mulattas, &c. The money, unless altered in value, is so much below sterling, that an English shilling goes for 7s. and a Spanish pistarine for the same; 4d. for half a crown currency, and 1½d. for a shilling; so that their currency is 700 per cent beneath the lawful money of Great Britain. Charles-Town harbour is spacious, being a kind of large cove almost land-locked, and receiving the falls of Ashley river, Joseph's river, and Cooper's or Hob-coe river; but the navigation is considerably impeded by a bar at the entrance between Sullivan's island and the main, where there is not above 3½ or 4 fathoms of water at the best tides, which never rise high. Oysters are so plentiful about the harbour, and especially Dog-island creek, that they throw them on heaps to rot, and then burn the shells for lime, which is excellent.

Dublin is the metropolitan city of the kingdom of Ireland: It is situate on the banks of the Liffay, over which there are some fine bridges. The streets are spacious, the buildings stately and magnificent, and the cathedral is dedicated to St. Patrick: Besides which, there are many very neat parish churches; also a fine castle, a guild-hall, tolcel, mansion-house, and a superb college which has scarcely its equal in the world; likewise two houses of parliament, where the Peers and Commons of the realm assemble for the dispatch of public business, under the auspicious authority of the Lord Lieutenant or Viceroy, whose residence is in the castle. This city is opulent and populous as well as splendid, and might vie with even London itself in point of commerce, was it not for their navigation being rather incommodious, on account of a bar, on which there are not more than 3 fathoms of water, or thereabouts, at high water, and often a great swell when the wind is easterly, which renders it dangerous, and even almost impassible in a gale: Notwithstanding,

when a vessel is over the bar, she is safe, as there is a good pier built
from King's-end to the bank on the south side of the channel: and
on the end of the said bank is a floating light, to give direction in
the night. The cove or harbour within the pier is called pole-beg;
and on the south side the river at the lower part of the town, are
several good quays, known by the names of John's, George's,
Austin's, coal and custom-house quay, where there is often a great
many vessels, in particular colliers of Whitehaven, Workington,
and Cockermouth; but King's ships and those on quarantine are
obliged to lie without the bar in the bay between Dunlary and the
Hill of Hoath, which is badly sheltered. The inhabitants of this city,
and indeed of Ireland in general, are courteous and humane, as
touching many things, such as relieving the wants of their fellow-
creatures, and other acts of hospitality; but when provoked, they
are fierce, cruel, impatient of revenge, bloody, and well-nigh sav-
age; not regarding the life of a man more than that of a beast, or
even a reptile of the most malignant nature. The river running
through the city, divides it into two almost equal parts, north and
south; they are sometimes distinguished by Liberty and Ormon,
which terms originated from that memorable contest which once
subsisted between the citizens, on a plan and proposals being
formed by the British legislature, and offered under the adminis-
tration of the Duke of Ormon, for abolishing the Irish parliament,
and bringing Ireland into a strict and close union with Great
Britain; on which, part accepting, and part excepting against the
proposals, a dangerous faction broke out, which was attended with
serious consequences, and threatened worse: Butchers turned out
with cleavers; carpenters with handsaws and axes; and others with
pitch-forks, fire-pokers, &c. making no spare of those they met
with of what rank or age soever, if they were not of their party, or
had not their watch-word; and where this contest would have
ended, God only knows, had not the proposals been withdrawn. In
one of these rencounters, the parties met on a bridge, where so
many were slain and thrown over into the Liffay, that it obtained
the name of Bloody-Bridge. The chief Magistrate is stiled Lord
Mayor, and the subordinate ones, Aldermen, Common-Council
Men, &c. The chief manufactures of this metropolis are silks,
poplins, cottons, and linens, which they export in great quantities to
different parts of the world.

Cork may, in some respects, be called the second city in the kingdom, and in point of commerce, perhaps the first; especially since the trade of Ireland is no longer circumscribed by acts of the British parliament: It is far inferior to Dublin, yet it is large and populous, though many of the houses, especially in the suburbs and out parts of the town, are mean to a proverb. Its manufactures are poplins, linens, &c. and in the adjacent parts of the country there are kept large dairies for butter, some of the graziers keeping 150 or 200 cows; and great numbers of horned cattle and hogs are bred and fed: They slaughter and cure abundance of provisions, and export beef, pork, and butter, for the supply of great part of our West India islands, His Majesty's Royal Navy, and the East India Company's ships, &c. the place being favoured with a very useful and eligible navigation; yet vessels of more than about 300 tons burden cannot get up the quays, but take in their lading at Passage, a village situate on the river 5 miles below the city: And 2 miles lower, is a very large and commodious lough or cove, entirely surrounded by land except a small entrance, and spacious enough to hold a very numerous fleet at safe anchorage, it being the best and most extensive harbour in the kingdom; although those of Kinsale and Limerick are very large and safe for great ships, and partly rival this place in merchandise. But notwithstanding their trade and commerce, the streets abound with beggars; and if you stop in the public parts of the town, you are sure to have a shoe-black brushing at your feet; for in the country adjoining, as indeed throughout the province of Munster, and perhaps the greatest part of Ireland, the lands lying chiefly in great men's hands, numbers of people who have not trades are destitute of employment, and subsist on little else than ferahauns and butter-milk, in inland places; but by the sea side, they get herrings and other fish to eat with their ferahauns, i.e. potatoes, if they can procure a boat to catch them in. Many of their huts or houses are only a mud wall run up about 5 or 6 feet high, and covered in at the top with straw or potato tops, having a hole in the side which serves for the use of a door, window, and chimney, which is barricaded in cold weather with a faggot. The fire is usually made in the middle of the floor, the smoke ascends through the thatch, and the family sit round to warm themselves, some almost naked except a piece of blanket wrapt round them, and barefoot, unless the Master and Mistress have

either of them a pair of brogues, which are a sort of shoes, but
sewed with thongs instead of thread. Those who are so rich as to
get a pig or cow are still under the disagreeable necessity of letting
it have one side of the fire; the family inhabiting one end of the
house, and the cattle the other: Their beds are likewise of one sort,
viz. straw. I do not assert this from hear-say, having had ocular
demonstration of the facts. On the north side of the cove there is a
smart little town which bears the name of Cove, or the Cove of
Cork: Lying here in the winter of 1760, with the *Hawke, Fox*, and
Boscowen, East Indiamen homeward-bound, our Officers were
somewhat concerned in smuggling India goods from them; and as
the cutter was coming down from Passage with the Doctor, the
wind taking her aback, she overset, and he launched overboard
head foremost (being fast asleep) as she was going over, and was
drowned: The rest getting on the boat's bottom and calling for
assistance, were heard from a merchant ship and taken off. The
boat was also saved, only she had lost her oars. One day after this,
our Captain, Lieutenants, and Master, with Captain Hume of the
Fox, &c. going ashore in the barge and cutter to shoot game, after
spending the greatest part of a winter's day to little purpose, we
drew near the mansion of Mr Fitzgerrald, a noted gentleman of an
opulent fortune, who had given our gentlemen an invitation to supper: The boats' crews were also called in and placed at the second
table, which was spread with plenty; but I and another going in
after the rest, were placed at a table by ourselves, where we were
regaled with only herrings and potatoes. We had undoubtedly reason to be thankful for such hospitality, yet we could not help
envying our shipmates, whom we saw entertained with roast beef,
mutton, fowls, greens, &c. However we would not be so rude as to
refuse what was set before us, not yet remove to the other table, but
were at a loss how to unravel the mystery; inferring from it, that the
servants supposed us prejudiced against flesh on that day, it being
Friday, because we stayed behind till called a second time; but men
of war's men are never so superstitious as they might imagine. The
currency of Ireland is under sterling, so that an English guinea goes
for 1l. 2s. 9d. a half crown for 2s. 8½d. and a shilling for 13d. The
nobility, gentry, and commonalty, dress much as they do in
England, only the women of the latter class seldom wear stays, hats,
or pattens; and many of the men wear brogues instead of shoes.

I shall say no more of Liverpool than that it is an exceeding fine town, situate on the north bank of the river Mersey, and the third mercantile sea-port in the kingdom, (although the navigation is difficult by reason of the sands at the fall of the river shifting by the force of the tides) because my reader may have an opportunity of visiting it without venturing himself within the thickness of a four-inch plank of a watery grave.

The lsle of Man is a small island situate in the Irish channel in an angle, between England, Scotland, and Ireland, the chief town of which is Castle-town; but Douglas having a tolerable good bay, is the most populous, and has the greatest trade, being a safe road for large ships. This island was formerly a refuge for rogues, and a nest for smugglers; as the former were out of danger from sheriffs' officers, and the latter from tide-waiters; it being a place of free trade, and not subject to our laws, except for capital crimes. The title of royalty or king, in Man, with some revenue, was for many years enjoyed by the Stanley's family, earls of Derby; but the male line of that family becoming extinct, it was transferred to the Duke of Athol by a female branch of the Stanleys' marrying into the Murrays' family: And in the beginning of the present reign, the royalty was given up to His Majesty, and the island made subject to the laws of England. The inhabitants are called Manksmen; their language seems to be a compound of Herse and Irish, as a Manksman can understand either an Highlander or Irishman.

Quebec is the capital of the vast province of Canada in North America: It is situate on a point between the river St Lawrence and the north river, where the latter river falls into the former. This capital surrendered to the British forces employed against it under the joint command of Generals Wolfe, Townsend, and Murray, and Admirals Saunders, Durel, and Holmes, on the 13th of September, 1759; though before it was taken possession of by the victors, the command of the land forces devolved on General Townsend by the death of the brave General James Wolfe, who expired on the bed of honour from a wound he had received at the beginning of the attack on the plain of Abraham. For the particulars of the siege, I refer my reader to Dr Entick's history of the German war, and only say, that this once splendid city remained in a ruinous condition, having suffered very much from the bombardment and cannonading of the English during the siege; and having again been besieged, in the course of the winter, by the French, who had not only battered the back parts of the town which had escaped the shot and shells in the former siege, but by erecting a battery of heavy ordnance on the ice in the river, had done much additional damage to the front of the buildings; so that there remained only the bare outside shells of stately stone-built houses, while every thing combustible about them was consumed; and scarce one public or private building in the place left tenable, except the nunnery and convent; the former, after releasing the nuns, being converted into an hospital for the English sick and wounded soldiers, and the latter into a magazine for the stores and provisions. These, and some few more which stood but little exposed, were left entire, while the residue were either made skeletons, or their sides perforated by the shot and pieces of shells, so that they might be seen through; and large concave places like horse-ponds might be seen in the streets, where shells had fallen and danced about before they burst. The Governor's house standing on an eminence much exposed to the be siegers, exhibited a striking spectacle, being quite full of holes the whole length of the wall. – Such are the effects of that diabolical traffic, war!!! A little below the citadel, is a remarkable water-fall, where the whole stream of the river Merancy, being about 100 yards wide, falls off Montgomerancy at least 60 feet perpendicular into the river St Lawrence, the noise of which may be heard many leagues off. The river is navigable for ships of the largest draught of water, as high as Quebec; for frigates and merchant ships, as far as Trois Riveris; and for small craft, to Montreal; whence they bring abundance of furs and peltry. The water purging itself by its continual flux and reflux, is perhaps the best river water in the world, except the Thames, particularly for keeping sweet at sea. The tide runs very rapid, especially on the ebb, as it receives the fall of many small rivers, and the conflux of the lakes Champlain and Ontario, so that it ordinarily runs at about 9 or 10 knots; and in some of the straits, such as that between coudre and the main, sometimes at the rate of 12 or 14. The current descending from Lake Ontario has in its course several falls from rocks of considerable height, one of which is, perhaps, the greatest in the universe. The cold here is so intense in winter, that the rivers are always frozen up (notwithstanding the rapidity of the tides) so as to bear almost any weight; and snow is frequently as high as the walls;

and to prevent the inroads of the French while they were investing it, the men were, with infinite labour, obliged to throw it away in the nights, by which many of them lost the use of their hands. Canada produces great quantities of excellent grain, in particular, wheat, barley, and maize; also vegetables: Many parts of it abound with wood and timber, such as fir, pine, live-oak, and spruce; the latter is of two sorts, viz. white and black; the branches of which make good beer. In these woods are found wild beasts of various kinds, and some reptiles of an enormous size. The inhabitants are a mixture of French, English, and Canadian Indians, who, respecting habit and sentiment, partly adhere to the customs they have been wonted to; yet in articles of cloathing, they need something of a better defence against the cold in winter than we; their seasons being much more severe, although they are not so far north. This province is rendered considerable by its commerce, the chief article of which is furs, which they purchase of the Indians, whose itinerant tribes travel about for the purpose of hunting; sometimes carrying with them slight materials to erect wigwams where it best suits their convenience; though often their squaws and pickininies, i.e. wives and children, are destitute of any other shelter than what a thick bush affords them. In winter they screen themselves from the cold by the use of bear-skins and beaver-skins, which also serve them for bedding in the night as well as cloathing in the day, always using them with the fur side next their skin; but at other times they go naked, painting their skins green, when the trees are verdant; and brown, when the leaves are off; to correspond with the woods in which they range; accounting clothes an incumbrance. Some of them wear a bob at their nose, and most of them slit the flaps of their ears and decorate them with plumes of various colours. In their ceremony of marriage, the man presents the woman with a haunch of venison, in token that he will provide meat by hunting in the woods; and she, in return, gives him a full head of maize, to signify that she will plant, and so support him and their pickininies with bread; and thus the wedding is completed without any more bustle or expence, as they seldom have a house, and consequently need no furniture; for being at best but fugitives, and wood being plentiful wherever they sojourn, it is easy to erect a wigwam to serve their present occasion; and when they please, they abandon it, and remove to another place they like better; and that they may not be impeded in their route by the rivers, they construct canoes of birch bark and a small matter of wood, sewing them with fibres, and peying them with gum: These are light enough to make them portable, so that having ferried themselves over one river, they carry the canoe along with them to another. They are very alert and active; exceeding fond of liquor; and when inebriated, revengeful, vindictive, and cruel; so that when their squaws perceive them to have got too much, they hide all their knives and other offensive weapons, left they should, in their fury, murder either them or their pickininies. If a family has lost any relations in battle, they are not satisfied till they have revenged the loss in the destruction of as many of their enemies. They are of a dark cedar-colour complexion; mostly eat raw flesh; and when in want of provision, will go out and shoot a deer or other beast, and cut a piece and eat it while it is warm and tough; leaving the rest for the wolves and bears to eat. My continuance here did not afford me the opportunity of an immediate acquaintance with them, and their way and manner of life; but I obtained a very minute and particular account of them from Mr George Abel, the yeoman of our sheats, who had been 18 months a prisoner amongst them, and had travelled about with an Indian family. An old man and his two sons belonging to a war-like tribe, which had covenanted with the French to serve in the war, on condition that if one or more of them fell in battle, the relations of each family respectively should have their numbers made up again from among the prisoners, if they took any: And George, serving on the lake Ontario with Captain Leforey, late Admiral Sir John Leforey, was taken at Oswago and given by the French to replace a youth of the above mentioned family, who had been killed by Captain Leforey's sloop, in the engagement. His adoption into this itinerant tribe exposed him to the greatest hardships imaginable, being painted, obliged to eat raw meat, &c. and many times enduring cold, hunger, and fatigue; but the most he suffered was from the Indian father's resentment for refusing to have his ears slit and decorated with plumes, as a necessary qualification for him having the young squa, an only daughter, who was passionately fond of him, and her brother also was his true and faithful friend; so that when ever the old man assayed to scalp him, which was very often, they rescued him by getting between him and their father, whose behaviour they watched attentively when he had got drink. But at length on coming to Montreal, he remonstrated with the Governor on the hardship of his case, being entitled to better treatment as a prisoner of war to the subjects of the most Christian King, &c. and was taken from them and put into prison; which being perceived, they set up a crying, and made such a tumult as obliged the guard to remove him into another prison, and allow them to search for him until they were weary; and finding themselves cheated, they went away yelling: After which, he was sent down to Quebec, where he obtained leave to work in the small craft, till the men of war sailing, brought him to Brest; and after remaining some time prisoner there, he was sent thence in a cartel vessel and pressed at Dartmouth before he landed. Before I take leave of Quebec, I shall take notice, that having a leisure hour, I, with two others of the boat's crew, went to the nunnery, which not being wanted any longer for an hospital, was reverted to its former use, to as many of those sequestered virgins as chose that kind of retired life, who were allowed protection and by no means to be molested, but at full liberty to dispose of themselves as they pleased, and were not under the superintendency of any priests or father-confessors, &c. as before. This building is very large and spacious, having an elegant chapel adjoining, to which the nuns could at any time go without the inconveniency of going out of doors. On the back side of it was a commodious garden and orchard, into which these recluse maidens sometimes retired for recreation, under the inspection of their matron; but these were surrounded by a very high wall, so that the poor girls were entirely cut off from any society or converse with, and almost from the sight of any person of the contrary sex, except those men of extraordinary sanctity the priests, friars, father-confessors, &c. and on necessary occasions, a physician or surgeon, when either health or limbs were in danger. The front of the building was ornamented with an emblematical piece of carved work, being the figure of a young woman having a dart stuck in her breast, to represent, I suppose, the anguish and extreme mortification of a keen though fruitless desire corroding the mind, without any, even the most distant prospect of ever having that desire gratified. Along the front was a large portico or piazza, the entire length of which was a kind of bulk's head instead of a wall: In this barricado were several holes or kind of ports, of different sizes, and in those were a sort of hollow tubes or vessels, having two entire ends with only half a bulge, which were so fixed as to turn round in the holes in such a manner, that when the convex or round side was outward, it entirely blocked up the space, and when the concave or hollow side was turned out, those on the outside might put any thing (not too large) into it, and turning it round they could get it on the inside; but when any of these were about half open, a person might peep in, and even converse with those who were within. We perceiving a rope hang out, pulled at it, which ringing a bell, soon brought one of the nuns; who opening a port, asked what we wanted? we said, to see the place; but she not knowing what we meant, went away; and returning, brought a little girl who spoke very good English: On her asking our business, we said, to buy some artificial flowers, by way of excuse; and on the young woman's retiring to fetch some, we begged of the little girl to ask leave for our admittance into the house: She said, I dare not, for the nuns will beat me; but if you go round the corner and turn on your right hand, you will find a door open, and may come in if you please. On the the young woman's returning, she shewed us many curious flowers of various forts, very dexterously wrought indeed: We asked the price of several, but not wanting any, they were all too dear; and at length being weary of such bad customers, she retired with them. We, according to the information received from our little friend within, pursued our intended excursion; and finding the door open, went in; then going up stairs, viewed first one spacious apartment and then another, all of which were then deserted, and only some lumber left in them, till at length we came to a very large room where a grave old matron sat teaching some girls, among whom was our little interpreter: On our appearance, the old lady rose up, and with seeming very great indignation, bid us be gone; and on our appearing not to understand what she said (for she spoke French) or if we did, not regarding it, she was exasperated to the last degree, and threatened to make her remonstrance to the Commodore; on which we, to avoid any disturbance, withdrew, leaving the old woman raging; and I have never since enquired how she settled. Before I take my leave of this place, I shall observe, that these nuns are such as, either by their own voluntary choice, or by their parents' arbitary disposal of them, are secluded, as afore mentioned, from any intercourse with any but their own sex except as above – As though sequestration from an object was sufficient to kill innate desires, or take away an habitual passion of the mind, and destroy the natural appetite of the body; a proof of the contrary is evident to a demonstration, from the great tenderness shewn by those of them who acted as nurses to the sick and wounded while the nunnery was an hospital; and the major part of them accepting the overture of liberty held out to them by the conquerors, as well as great numbers of them marrying among the English soldiers.

Hamburg is situate on the River Elbe, and is a city of some consequence in the mercantile world, having a considerable share of trade with this and several other countries of Europe: It adjoins to Low Germany and Denmark, yet is neither subject to the Emperor nor the King, but is a free city and a small common wealth of itself; always obliged, like other little republics, to observe a strict neutrality, let whoever will be at war; so that the want of power preserving peace, and promoting industry, becomes at once the means of accumulating and keeping wealth as well as domestic happiness and respectability with its neighbours.

Batavia is the chief city in the island of Java, and the emporium of all the Asiatic trade of the Dutch East India Company, as also the rendezvous of their ships, where they arrive first from Europe and take their orders from the company's Commodore; who, as chief director of their extensive commerce in India, sends them thence, some to the Grooht Oste and Klyne Oste, and others to Japan, China, Malacca, Bengal, Sumatra, Ceylon, Nagapatam, Poulacat, various parts on the gulf of Persia, and on the coast of Malabar, with almost every other part of Asia. Most of the ships so sent out return hither again richly laden with the produce of the places to which they were respectively sent, which is landed and lodged in this grand depository of commercial wealth, from whence it is again shipped for the Netherlands. The city is very extensive; the houses are built on handsome constructions, large, and with spacious windows, neatly glazed, in front: They are of brick and flat tile, and generally without chimnies; so that there are no complaints of smoky houses; for the air being always hot, there is no need of artificial warmth: For cooking and other domestic uses, they have small out-houses in their yards, and some make their fire out of doors for such purposes. The streets are not paved, but are very spacious; all the principal ones of which have a canal, navigable for boats, running down the middle of them, so that they have water-carriage to steps facing their doors, with street-room enough on either side, and bridges at the junction of the cross-streets: And on each side many of these canals, there is a row of trees, which form agreeable shades, where benches are fixed for gentlemen to sit to drink and spend their evenings. Here is one large, and three small churches; to the former of which a poor person is hardly ever admitted. The bazar, or market-place, is very large and commodious, being most of it covered in with shades; it is always well supplied with meat, fish, fowls, fruits, and vegetables, which the shades preserve in good order, otherwise the sun and wind would soon spoil them. The citadel is encompassed with a wall and a ditch, with very heavy artillery mounted on the ramparts quite round it; and at the mouth of the canal, on the north side close to the water, they have a strong fort, which they call the water-castle, that commands the road; and in this, as well as the town, they have always a powerful garrison, so that they deem the place almost impregnable; and their soldiers, when on their posts, require homage from those who pass them. The road is safe and capacious enough to hold, perhaps, half the British navy at safe anchorage, being environed with a number of small islands, which they call after the names of some of their towns, &c. such as Amsterdam, Rotterdam, Flushing, Middleberg, Edam, Sceidam, Cooper's island, Lazarus's island (where they have an hospital for incurables, and a burying-ground) and Ondross, or Onrust, (where they have a very good arsenal of naval stores, with a wharf and every thing necessary for careening and heaving down ships) They have also store-houses, & c. on Cooper's island, which is hard by Ondross. These isles not only shelter the road, but supply the town with tortoise, with which they abound; while the inland waters swarm with large alligators, as voracious as any in the world. In this road the company's ships take in their cargoes, which are brought down in sampans and tanipores. They have generally two pretty large fleets sail from hence every year, the latter of which they call the sygar-schips, i.e. sugar-ships, because they always have a quantity of sugar and coffee on board, which they stow in their bottoms for dunage, to secure the more valuable articles from damage; the residue of their loading consists of black and white pepper, cloves, mace, cinnamon, nutmegs, fine cotton, various kinds of drugs, and

Japan copper, which is nearly as fine as gold; with some teas and raw silk; but their china trade is somewhat limited, on account of a piece of fraud and villany they were detected in by the Chinese manderines at Wampoa. They seldom bring any quantity of arrack home, lest it should spoil their Geneva distillery. This fleet sails about the latter end of October or the beginning of November; and as soon as the General and Commodore have respectively made up their several and joint accounts for the past year, they send them off in a single ship, which they call the brief schip, i.e. the packet or letter-ship: This vessel sails in February or March, and is sometimes so late as to be obliged to beat round the Cape in the depth of winter, when the wind is mostly contrary; yet the current generally setting in her favour, renders it practicable; nay, they will lay to in a gale of wind while the weather-current carries them round; for the harder it blows from the S. W. the stronger the stream runs, as before shewn. The Dutch East Indiamen are most of them 1400 or 1500 tons burden, and can mount 40 or 50 guns each in case of necessity. Batavia river is no better than a canal, there being not more than 5 or 6 feet of water on the bar, and very little tide, which occasions their dragging the boats and other small craft up with horses. The streets abound with neat hackney coaches, which are drawn by beautiful pairs of little stallions, and drove by Blacks or Malays. Rice boiled dry is much used here, as a substitute for bread, and good water is a very scarce article. The inhabitants are a composition of Europeans, Malays, Chinese, black Portuguese, and Caffrees; I shall say a little of each in order – The Europeans are most of them Netherlanders, with some few of almost every other nation: These are very differently situated; the Governor (who is also Generalissima of the company's forces) takes as much state, and affects almost as much grandeur as any sovereign prince in Europe; insomuch that when he in his carriage meets another gentleman, he requires him to stop, alight, and stand bare-head while he is passing. He has command of all their different corps stationed in their several Indian settlements and factories, and superintends all their cantonments, posts, and movements; having the direction of all their military operations in this quarter of the globe; and to him the several returns of every subordinate governor and military commander is made, and by him transmitted to the court of directors in Holland: His continuance in office is 3 years, and while in that station he is assisted by a second commandant, whom they call Vice-Gall or Sub-Governor. The Commodore too is in great power; and this port being made the centre of all their eastern commerce, he not only directs the whole of it, but holds the inferior officers in the greatest submission; so that when he goes on board of a ship to give his orders, he is met at the gangway by the Captain, who stands with his hat off all the while he is on the quarter-deck: He is assisted in his office by a Vice-Commodore, and sometimes a third in command, whom they call Vice-Vice-Commodore. The European grandees here wear light suits resembling their respective mother countries, with this difference, that in the cold fens of Holland and the other united provinces, they are glad to keep their hats on their heads to prevent a running at the nose; but here, they walk in the streets with them under their arms, to avoid the trouble of frequently taking them off, as it is customary for them to bow to every gentleman they meet or pass; and to avoid the disagreeable effects which might arise from this, they have each a black boy or man, who walks behind them and carries a kedifall over their heads; and woe be to any of them if they suffer the sun to shine on the face of their masters: The kedifall is a sort of large umbrella, fixed on a long staff to enable the kedifallboy to vary his position as occasion may require. Here are very few white women, consequently those few are much esteemed, and have great attendance; they are seldom seen in the streets except in a carriage. The officers and soldiers are obliged to wear their respective uniforms, notwithstanding the inconvenience of such habiliments, in extreme hot weather. The mates and petty officers belonging to ships in the road frequently wear full suits of light clothes, except shirts, which they some of them go without, although they wear two pair of breeches, with gold or silver buttons in the waistband linked together like those for a shirt sleeve; but the common matrosses, i.e. seamen, many of them wear only a cap and a pair of trowsers, except what we were wont to call a Batavia jacket, viz. a sun-burnt skin: Numbers of these poor fellows fall a sacrifice to the climate, and the rigorous treatment of their officers; I have seen some of them, for trifling offences, stand between two Quarter-Masters, who, with each a piece of $2\frac{1}{2}$ inch rope, beat them on the back, stroke for stroke, like thrashers, till they have fallen at their feet – this they call the bel-flahn. Their provision is generally so bad and scanty, that they expend their wages in adding something to it. They are engaged variously; some boys at 5 guilders per month, for 9 years service; others at 7 guilders, for 7 years; youths and ordinary seamen at 9 guilders, for 5 years; and able seamen, &c. at 12 guilders, for 3 years; but often when their time is drawing to a conclusion, the Commodore will order them on board some ship bound to Amboyna and Banda, or to Japan, &c. so that being absent when the fleet sails, they miss their turn, and must wait some future opportunity. Their outward-bound ships mostly carry about 500 men, including soldiers, (who are released at the expiration of 5 years) and seldom muster more than about 100 when they leave the country to return. The Malays are the natives of this and some of the neighbouring islands; they are in general of a middle stature, well proportioned, strong made, and would be extremely handsome if mature had been so profusely bountiful as to bless them with as agreeable complexions as the natives of some of the northern nations of Europe, yet though they are not fair, neither are they black, but a kind of reddish brown or copper-colour: They are robust and very active, making good soldiers. Some of the men wear light thin clothes, agreeable to their climate; while others wear only a kind of sash round their loins, so disposed as to cover their nakedness; it is mostly a piece of cotton cut off the web and wrapped round them, and the end tucked in to fasten it. The women wear a sort of single petticoat and short waistcoat without sleeves, or but very short ones, and no shift; They are never troubled with cleaning their shoes, neither have they ever any corns on their feet; nor do they affect to appear with a head much larger than nature intended, for their decoration is very simple; they oil and comb their long black hair, then thrust a pin 4 or 5 inches long through a lock on the crown, and then roll the hair round under the pin so as to make it lie flat and resemble a small truck. The Chinese, who compose a considerable part of the inhabitants of this populous city, and especially of the suburbs, are the descendants of those of that nation who fled hither first as refugees when their own country was invested by the Tartars, and afterward settled and became naturalized Javans, rather than submit to the Tartar princes and Tartarian laws when China was conquered by the great Cham of Tartary, who, on that acquisition, obtained the magnificent title of Cham of Tartary, Emperor of China, and King of 10000 islands.

These people differ much from the former, as their make and constitutions are not so hale and robust; but their very frame and appearance shew weakness and indigence; their complexions are sickly, and exhibit a moving image of death, the colour of their faces being like the pale part of lignumvitæ; yet they, like the rest of the human species, over-fond of themselves, suppose they are extremely beautiful, and will accordingly say to Europeans, 'you want pretty face, you bring pretty face.' The men pluck the hairs from their beards, leaving only here and there a straggling one on their chins; shave their heads very clean all over except a single lock on the back side of the crown, which they let grow to its full length; and generally go without hats, though some of them wear one of a very aukward construction: They keep the nails of their two middle fingers pared close, but never pare those of the thumb, fore, and little fingers, except it be such as cannot suffer them to grow on account of their employment. The women wear a thin petticoat and a loose gown, but seldom any thing of covering for the head except what nature has furnished them with: They oil and comb their hair, and wear it in sleek and loose tresses. Those of both sexes wear a kind of shoes, or rather slippers, which would be perfect shackles on the feet of an European. They are an industrious, lively, and active people, notwithstanding the delicacy of their constitutions, and exceedingly ingenious in many useful manufactures: They always write in characters or short hand marks, each representing a word; yet some say they have more characters in use than their language contains words: They use India ink, and always hold their pencil in the hand as we do a stick, with the thin edge of the hand downward, and begin at the top of the page, writing down to the bottom. They, and indeed their whole nation, a few excepted, are a set of the most accomplished thieves upon the face of the earth, the Russians and Tartars not excepted; they steal, and encourage others to do so; they buy stolen goods, and take every advantage in buying, selling, &c. to cheat, go beyond, and defraud any person they have concern or dealing with: Knavery is so prevalent and habitual among them, that they will plead custom for it instead of law, as one of them once did with Commodore Anson at Wampoa; who, after receiving repeated favours from the Commodore, had employed some of his servants to steal a top-mast from under the stern of the *Centurian*; and on the Commodore's expostulating with him about such a disingenuous piece of behaviour to his benefactor, he excused it by the custom of his country, saying, 'Chinamen very great rogue truly, but have fashion no can help.' Yet however they may be disesteemed by others, they esteem themselves the wisest people in the world, and value themselves greatly on this very account, as though they thought all other nations and people fools in comparison to themselves. They use serpents very much in their paintings, and in the form of their vanes at their mast heads; also portray large eyes on the bows of their vessels, &c. as hieroglyphics of their superior sagacity above others; from whence they say a Chinaman has three eyes, a Dutchman two, and an Englishman one. They are not in any wise a martial people, but as on the afore mentioned principle they make haste to be rich, by using every means, fair and unfair, they frequently accumulate much wealth: And as their Dutch governors love money as well as they do, and pay as little regard how they come at it, they might perhaps as well have submitted to the new form of government in China at the revolution; for when they have collected an abundance of treasure, the Dutch generally pretend some information or suspicion of conspiracy or treason against government, which they make the ground of a quarrel; and have sometimes carried it so far as to exasperate the Chinese into a transport of rage, until at last, after having smoked bang and opium sufficient to benumb their senses and feelings, and carry them on almost to a degree of madness, they, under that stupor and rage, would murder any person they met in their way; and then, after pronouncing their watchword, amuck! amuck! they have actually made insurrection, and killed or maimed some person or persons in the streets; which overt acts have been deemed sufficient to confirm their suspicions, (though at first neither founded on truth nor justice) and to justify them in falling on the insurgents and cutting them off by military execution, and seizing on their property as confiscated by their rebellion. The black Portuguese are, by extraction, Moors and Gentoos, but have been brought to embrace christianity by the Portuguese missionaries, as well as to have learned something of that language, which is in part spoken all over India; so that if a man can speak Portuguese, he may find some who can understand him on any part of the continent, and in most of the island: These people are free, and follow trades, habiting themselves like the Dutch, amongst whom they dwell. The Caffrees derive their denomination from Caffria in Africa, the natives of which country have short woolly hair like the Negroes, although these are most of them slaves imported from Madagascar and Johanna: With respect to their dress, I shall only say, they do not go entirely naked as many slaves do in our West India islands; and from the manner in which they treat their seamen, I will leave my reader to infer how these are treated by their masters. This is not a place of free commerce, but entirely in the power of the Dutch East India Company, and under the governance of their General and Commodore; so that no merchant or other person can trade in the city, or even in the parts adjacent, without a license first had and obtained from the said officers respectively, enabling them so to do. Here are 12 arrack-houses or distilleries, and as this sort of liquor is peculiar to this part of the globe, I shall say something about it: It is distilled from rice, molasses, and cocoa-nut wine or milk (which is a liquid contained in the middle of a cocoa-nut) and is as fine and wholesome as any rum, and of a better flavour, though on account of its cheapness, it is often drank too freely, and hurts European constitutions: I have bought it at Chinese punch-houses for two stivers a bottle, and large quantities may be purchased cheaper: There is a great deal of it made at Goa, by the Portuguese, and at Columba, by the Dutch, but none to equal that at Batavia, either for strength or flavour. The monsoons here are not so much periodical winds as wet and dry seasons, the former of which sometimes lasts from September till April, when the rains fall in abundance, attended with thunder and lightning; but the trade-wind mostly prevails in its due course in the day-time; yet I have known a westerly wind continue for 6 or 8 weeks together, and sometimes very variable; at other times, in particular during the dry monsoons, the sea-breeze dies away in the evening, and a sultry land-breeze succeeds a short calm, and continues till about 10 o'clock in the morning, when the sea-breeze comes in and blows strong, which is so refreshing that it may be called the doctor with as much propriety as at Jamaica: Before this breeze gets strength, and particularly during the night, the people are very much annoyed with mosquitoes (little insects like our gnats or midges) which prevent them from sleeping; and sometimes the bite of one of them has, by being scratched, become an ulcer; and their venom is so very sharp, that it is soarely possible to avoid it: This I have seen; and have been told, that they have sometimes caused the amputation of a limb; for here a very slight hurt will often occasion a wound, which may get malignant, and sometimes fatal, as the blood is disordered and scorbutic, which may be attributed to various causes; first, the land adjoining to the city is very low and flat, and almost covered with wood, which hinders the air from having a free course; and the ground is nitrous and impregnates the air with vapours, and the water with an ill flavour and noxious tincture: Secondly, at the distance of only 37 Dutch miles, there grows the tree called, in the Malayan language, bohan-upas, which I suppose is the most poisonous plant in the world, as it entirely destroys the vegetation of 394240 acres of land which lie round it within the distance of 14 miles; its gum will affect steel, and the Malays in this island and Sumatra, Borneo, &c. with several places on the continent, have their warlike instruments touched with it, so that the slightest touch will affect the blood and cause almost instant death; and when those instruments are once insated with it, they will have the same fatal effect many years afterward: The effluvia arising from this tree impregnates the air so as to kill birds flying near it, and may help to render the whole island unhealthful: And thirdly, as the sun's rays have never any more than 29 deg. 40 min. obliquity in their direction, the atmosphere is always very hot; and when he is vertical, as on the 9th of October and 4th of March, it is intensely so; which days happening in the wet monsoons, great exhalations are raised from the nitrous earth, which conspire to ruin the constitution and destroy life. Twelve Dutch miles from this city, toward the straits, is the town of Bantam, which was formerly the capital of the island, at which place a number of English were cruelly massacreed some years ago: It is still a good town, though of but little trade, notwithstanding its bay is large and safe for a considerable fleet. Although the interior parts of Java form an empire and several kingdoms, yet the Dutch, by being in possession of Batavia and Bantam, absolutely give law to and accumulate the wealth of this flourishing and extensive island; for they arbitrarily demand its productions at their own price, as they generally do wherever they extend their influence in this part of the globe, and indeed scarce stick at any thing that may facilitate their aggrandizement and dominion: It produces various sorts of spice, and the low lands that encompass the city abound with excellent vegetables, and tropical fruits of all kinds, particularly annises or pineapples, and mangoes, which grow spontaneously; and the cocoa-nut tree is here made to serve for many uses, although in many places where they are plentiful, they serve but few: The tree itself is porous and spongy like the cabbage-tree, and only fit for making fashines after it is cut down, but while it is growing, they tap it, and catch the juice it emits, which while fresh, serves for barm to raise bread; when it is a day old, it is tolerable good beverage; and when 3 or 4 days old, it is indifferent vinegar: Of the shells they make cups, ladles, and other utensils; and of the fibres of the outward husks they make threads, and work them into caiau cables, hawsers, and other cordage, and even light sails for boats and prooas, as well as mats, &c. for domestic uses; and the kernel, as well as the milk, is used in victuals several ways. Some of their prooas here are built on so nice a construction, that they will sail at the rate of 24 miles an hour. The feathered tribes here are numerous; the greatest rarities amongst which, are the white cockatore or crocator, which very much resembles a tropic-bird, only he has a beautiful crown or crest on his head, and will talk like an African parrot; the lorie, which is the finest talking bird in the world, and of the most beautiful variegated plumage; and the paradise-fowl, which is also of various colours and very handsome. Of reptiles, there are none more common than the centipede and the scorpion, which makes it dangerous to sleep on the ground – I speak from experience, having been bit by the former, and stung by the latter, while asleep. The sun's zenith distance here, on the 21st of June, is 29 deg. 41 min. and on the 21st of December, 17 deg. 17 min. so that here is no such thing as cold; and the latter of those two days is here the longest day, which does not exceed 12 hours and 24 minutes. The sun is on this meridian 7 hours, 6 minutes, and 52 seconds before he reaches the meridian of London; and 12 hours, 13 minutes, and 20 seconds before he is on the meridian of Port Royal in Jamaica; so that 12 o'clock here being only 53 min. 8 sec. past 4 in the morning at London, and only 46 min. 40 sec. past 11 on the preceding evening at Port Royal, we may suppose the several inhabitants to be very differently engaged; for suppose the Asiatics to be getting their dinners, the Europeans would be some asleep and others getting to work, and the Americans but lately gone to bed. While we lay at

Cooper's island in the *Panther*, having occasion to go to bury a man on Lazarus's island, it happened that all our boats were employed away from the ship, and the gunner of a country ship coming on board occasionally, we borrowed his boat for that purpose; and having got the corpse into her, four of us, a midshipman, and two Lascars who belonged to her, put off; and on coming along side a little wharf at the landing-place, two of our men stepped on shore to take hold of the coffin; and setting the Lascars to hold the boat to, one forward and the other abaft, I and the other man were about to lift it up; and treading on the thwarts with such a weight in our arms, caused the boat to heel, by reason of which the coffin had like to have touched the Lascar in the stern-sheats; on which he instantly letting go the stern-fast, the boat swung off; and to avoid falling overboard ourselves, we were obliged to let the dead man fall into the water; however we recovered him and got him ashore, but were incommoded all the way to the burying ground by the water running out of the coffin down our backs; and when we had performed this last office of respect to our deceased ship-mate, on returning to the jetty we found the Lascar somewhat recovered from his fright: Some would think it was but a small matter for the coffin to have touched the man; but he would almost as soon have lost his life, as he would thereby have lost his cast or religion, and have been esteemed no better than a beast or reptile. Have we no superstition in England?

Fort St George is situate on the coast of Coromandel, and at about two miles distance is the town of Madrass-a-Patnam, as it is called by the natives, though we call it Madrass: It is the principal place on this coast belonging to the Honourable United East India Company, and indeed it is their chief settlement in India, except Calcutta and Bombay; the former in the kingdom of Bengal, and the latter on the coast of Malabar: The last mentioned place, though not of so much importance for commerce, is yet of very singular use to the Company for the convenience of building and docking their ships of war and grabbs, which are essentially necessary for the defence and security of their possessions in this part of the globe, and to protect their trade against the Marahtas and other pirates about the coasts. The town of Madras is well fortified, and has often repelled the force of numerous assailants; and the fort, in which most of the Europeans reside, is also a fortification of very considerable strength, but the sea is almost ready to undermine it, as it also invades the whole coast; for the surf runs so high and beats so hard on the beach, that it keeps perpetually washing away the ground, so that ships now ride at anchor where the bazar or market was once kept. This road is the rendezvous for His Majesty's ships on the Coromandel coast, and is a very good anchoring ground, but being badly sheltered, is unsafe in the monsoon time, which obliges them to retire to Bombay or Trincomale during that season, if war do not prevent: There is scarce any bay, but it is almost like riding in the open sea; and at the fine time of the year the surf runs so high and impetuous, that it is not practicable for a boat to land with any degree of safety, except the masula-boats, which are built on a very peculiar construction, and of such materials as render them flexible, and so very pliant as to yield to the beach when they strike on it, so that they are able to bear those shocks that would dash any other boat in pieces: They are generally wrought by Lascars and Cooleys, who can swim well; and a ship's boat coming to a grappling, they take the passengers from her and land them; in order to which, they pull the masula-boat in, and when she touches, they jump out, some on each side, and bearing her in their arms, launch her upon the beach clear out of the surf: These boats are wide and deep, being made of very tough materials, and sewed together, and the masula-men are very dexterous in managing them. As the fort is the principal residence of the Europeans, it contains many good buildings; and the Black Town too has a great number of elegant houses in it, in which a many very opulent black merchants live in great splendor. His Majesty's governor and the Company's supreme council direct all the affairs of this country, and their officers survey the weights and measures, and also state the prices of every species of provision that is sold in the bazar as well as what is carried about the streets. The adjacent country for many miles is low and flat, and affords very little wood of any sort; and as they have no other kind of fuel, except some kajan, it renders that article scarce and dear; yet the evil is not much felt, as it is very little wanted for more uses than to cook their victuals and order their clothes. Sometimes they have no rain for 5 or 6 months together, or at most, very little; but in the wet monsoons, it falls very heavy and for many days without much intermission: The ground does not burn in the dry weather, nor is it dirty in the wet. They have various kinds of fruits, but not in such plenty as in some other places on the coast; and at some distance in land there are rice-swamps, but much of that necessary article is imported from Bengal, from whence they also get some wheat, as other parts of India do from Surat and the Cape of Good Hope, yet rice generally supplies the place of bread, and if they had the convenient use of good mills to grind it on, it would make excellent bread, and serve every other purpose of the pastry cook. Here, and at several of the adjoining places, they manufacture and export great quantities of muslins, long clothes, handkerchiefs, gingams, and other sorts of cottons: These and other wearables and things reducible to that purpose are in general very cheap, because little will do, and some articles are not fit for exportation: I have bought a pair of shoes for 1½ fanams, which is only 4¾d of our money; and the chucklers, i. e. shoe-makers, hawk them about the streets and sell them at 2 fanams a pair, as a common market price. A pair of these shoes will last about two months in dry weather, but if it rain, it then becomes necessary to secure them from the wet, they being only made of sheep-skins badly dressed, and the soals of a piece of green hide coloured with beadle-nut; so that one shoe, worn in the wet, would soon expand to a size sufficient to hold both feet. Provisions are in general plentiful and cheap, so that you may have a whole sheep for a rupee, which is equal to 2s. 6d. of our money; and a chuckler may buy a sheep-skin for a doodee, 9 of which go for a fanam. The children of chucklers and other manufacturers are here religiously obliged to follow their fathers' respective occupations, on pain of losing their cast. When gentlemen and ladies are disposed to indulge themselves with an easy ride, they may be better accommodated here than in England, as they may make use of a nice machine called a pallenkeen, which is slung and carried on a bamboo on the shoulders of two men: This vehicle is so contrived, that the person can either sit up or lie down, at pleasure. A little detached from Black Town is St Thomas's mount, which is a considerable height, where tradition says, St Thomas suffered martyrdom. The company have always a respectable force here, consisting of artillery and infantry, including a number of seapoy regiments, this being the place-de-arms for all their territorial acquisitions on this side the peninsula. The seapoy regiments are mostly commanded by an English officer, and will stand by him till they are cut off to the last man. The inhabitants are a mixture of English and other Europeans, Malabars, Moors, Gentoos, Armenians, black Portuguese, Bramines or Bracmans, and some Cafres. With respect to their several modes of dress and appearance, they are various: White women being rarities in India, I shall say nothing of them; and the European gentlemen being many of them officers and soldiers, are obliged to wear their respective regimentals; while clerks and others wear light suits of Indian man-ufacture, but commonly resembling the mode of dress in their mother country. The Moors and Gentoo men wear large earrings long enough to turn up over the top of the ear, which they do occa-sionally; and turbands, such as are usually worn by the Turks, Arabians, and Persians: They wear no shirts, but drawers and long white gowns or vests, which reach down to their feet, and gird them round their waists with a sash or girdle: Their shoes are made to turn up at the toes, resembling those worn in Poland; some are red and others green. Some of the Lascars and Coolies differ only in one small article of dress from the garb in which Adam and Eve appeared in the garden of Eden; yet the Coolies sometimes besmear themselves over with cocoa-nut oil and beadle-nut dust, which they think adds to their comeliness. Many of the women wear only a piece of cotton cloth variegated with colours cut off the web, one end of which they wrap round them as a petticoat, bring the other part over their breasts, then over their shoulders, and tuck it in at their waists. The Gentoos are very ingenious and industrious, and many of their women would be exquisite beauties if they were not black, as they have handsome features and excellent hair, &c. The Moors and Portuguese are exceeding black, and of various statures: And the Bramines are a sort of magicians or prognosticators, and a great deference is paid to their authority by many of the Asiatics, who reverence them, and strictly regard their prognostications as divine; hay even some Europeans have shewn much respect to some of their predictions; but some years ago, the governor of Nagapatam arrested two of these prophets as being false ones, and one of them was sentenced to suffer death by starving in a prison, and the other by being placed where a drop of water might fall on the crown of his head every 3 or 4 seconds, which brought on death by hydrophobia: The Bramines pay adoration to a voracious kite; and some of the afore mentioned people have Swamies, which they carry through the streets on elephants.

The Cape of Good Hope is situate near the southern extremity of that country which was once known by the name of Ethiopia-exteria, but is now called Caffraria, though some limit this denomination to the country situate more to the eastward, and bordering on the Indian ocean: It is large and beautiful: the houses are built low, and the walls washed with chinnam, which is much fairer than our Spanish white, and most of them are thatched with a kind of black rushes, which serve as a foil to the walls, and add much to their beauty. The staht-hoyse or town-hall is a very elegant building, of a square form, and flat roofed, situate in the middle of the staht, i. e. the town, and the streets spacious and regular. About a mile distance from the east side of the town is an eminence of considerable height, called the Table-Land, which is an entire rock quite flat at the top and many yards plumb on the side next the town, somewhat resembling a table with a close frame, from whence it takes its name. Off this high land the winds at times blow so impetuously, that they almost bear down every thing before them, which renders it necessary to build low, and keep the buildings in good repair. The promontary itself, which gives name to the place, is 35 miles to the southward of it; and between it and the staht there is a mountain of very great altitude and beauty, which, from the form of it, is called the sugar-loaf; on the top of it they have a flat-staff erected and keep a look out, and display their signals both to the town and ocean; and the height of this mount gives such a prospect, that scarce any thing in the offing can escape their notice. The bay is deep and very commodious, and abounds with fish of various kinds, and the adjacent country has not its equal in the world; it affords every substantial article necessary for the support of life, grain of all sorts in particular; great quantities of exceeding fine wheat, perhaps nothing inferior to the best in England: It abounds with choice vineyards, and affords fruits and vegetables of almost all kinds, not only such as we call tropical, but such as this and every other country in Europe produce. The Dutch boors, i. e. farmers, have extended their cultivation 500 miles up into the country, but are often alarmed by the natives, who rob their houses and farm yards, &c. which obliges them to have a strong guard. Horned cattle are plentiful and much used in the draught, which makes the beef generally coarse. Their sheep are very large, and of the Turkish kind; some of their tails weigh from 5 to 7 or

8lb. of entire fat (which is sometimes made into gee or butter) and are from 6 to 9 inches broad at the upper end: The mutton is generally about a stivre per lb. of 20 0z. and their wines, which are as good as any in the world, are white for 6d. and red for 8d. a bottle at the wine-houses. Bread, fish, fruits, and vegetables, are proportionably cheap, and always plentiful; but wood, the only fuel they have, is very dear: And clothing and other necessaries are obtained from Holland, which rather enhances their price. Here is the largest, most commodious, and elegant tyne or garden in the universe, which produces every kind of fruit, &c. in abundance; and where also the Company have kept a great variety of extraordinary and curious beasts and birds, particularly a number of ostriches; and also many sorts of serpents and reptiles: Into this tyne any stranger may be admitted, but is forbidden to touch any thing without leave, by an emblem fixed over the gate; which is a man stretching forth his hand to a tree, and another chopping his arm off with an axe. This country affords zibras and rhinocerases, the latter of which are stronger than an elephant; and although smaller, they are more hardy and robust: One of these being yoked to a ship that was overset in the bay, drew her upright. The longest day here is the 21st of December, when the sun's meridian altitude is 79 deg. 34 min. and the shortest day the 21st of June, when his zenith distance is 57 deg. 24 min. This place being in the southern temperate zone, of course their seasons are opposite to ours; the harvest is mostly got in January and February, and the vintage in February and March. The winter is never very severe, though they have both snow and frost; but the winds frequently blowing from the W. and N. W. during that season, renders it very unsafe for a Ship to lay in Table-bay: Those winds blowing directly on the shore, if her anchors do not hold her, there is no other alternative but inevitable destruction; on which account they strike the flag-staff on the 16th of May, and do not erect it again till the 16th of August, and during that interval do not suffer their own ships to come in on any account, but make those outward-bound proceed to the bay of False, and those homeward-bound to Sandana bay, where each are safe, and can get supplies of what they want. The Cape being about 2100 leagues from Holland, and 1900 from Batavia, serves as a half-way house, and is of the greatest utility to the Netherlands' Company for victualling their ships and supplying their eastern colonies with wheat, wine, &c. and whence they bring some wines home to the Netherlands. The inhabitants consist of Dutch, Germans, and other Europeans, with a number of Madagascarian and Cafre slaves; for a description of whose manners, dress, &c. see Batavia; only this being situate in a higher latitude, requires some better defence to secure them against the cold. The natives are Hottentots, who, by the Dutch, are driven far back into the interior parts of the country: They are a people of the lowest genius among the human race (unless it be those of Terra-del-Fuego) they are extremely indolent and slovenly, and have many ways so singular and alto-gether extraordinary, that I shall forbear to relate them, as my incredulous countrymen might from thence be led to doubt my veracity; I shall therefore refer them to the perusal of the accounts given by those gentlemen whose fortune and figure in the world give weight to their authority, and content myself with only observ-ing that they have never more than two fashions, which commence and go out alternately every half year; in the summer season they go naked, and in the winter they use a sheep's skin, sewing up the shanks for sleeves, and wear it as a waistcoat, with the hair side inward (for it scarcely can be called wool) to shelter them from the cold: A few of these live among the Dutch. The Portuguese were the first Europeans who discovered this country in exploring their passage to the East Indies, who, having coasted along shore a great many leagues, on passing the Cape, which they supposed to be the southermost point of the continent of Africa, and that now nothing remained to obstruct their proceeding to the eastward, exultingly called it Cape Bon Esperance, i. e. Cape of Good Hope, thinking that now they should soon arrive in the Indian ocean: They were not far mistaken; for Cape Falsa, which is the southern extremity of this continent, is only 4 miles more to the southward.

St Helena is a little island in the southern Atlantic, which being situate nearer the African continent than that of America, is called an African island: It belongs to the English East India company, to whom it is singularly useful, as its situation renders it most conve-nient for their homeward-bound ships to touch at for water and other necessaries, and to refresh their crews; it serves also for a ren-dezvous for them in time of war, where they usually collect together and lie till a sufficient force arrive to escort them safe to Europe: It is an entire rock farther detached from other land than any other island in the world, it is well fortified by nature, being inaccessible for a boat every where but on the N. W. where there is a good bay, and a neat small town called James-Town, which is exceedingly well secured by art, and garrisoned with the Companys' forces: This isle is a considerable height, and its cliffs are so full of large cavities, that a gun being fired in the bay, the report will echo from one to another as though 9 or 10 had been fired in succession. The surface is rather flat, and affords tolerable good pasture for cattle, with some fruits and vegetables, in particular celery and callilue, which grow spontaneously, tho' some part of it is volcanic; but though they have cattle, they are chiefly confined to live on salt provisions, by being obliged to furnish King's ships and homeward-bound India ships with fresh meat during their stay here; so that bullocks' lights are sometimes accounted a delicacy or extraordinary choice mess: Neither can any man dispose of his own property; but if he kill a pig, he must first acquaint the Governor, who allows him what part he pleases out of it, then disposes of the remainder amongst the town's people, and returns the owner the money, every such thing being reckoned public stock; yet the bay abounds with fish, which they may have for catching, such as albacore, bonetta, conger, and mackerel, which are very plentiful, particularly the latter, but it requires to be used quite fresh; else it soon becomes very gross, from the ground being copperish: They have also potatoes like ours, at 5s. per bushel, or 1s. 3d. per peck. However this little fertile island cannot be equaled in the universe for its salubrious air and singular situation, although in the torrid zone; yet being in the midst of the S. E. trade, they never want a refreshing breeze; and on the other hand never feel the force of a storm; and being high and surrounded by the sea, they are always free from disagreeable exhalations, mists, and fogs. The inhabitants are either Europeans, native Creoles, or Madagascarians. Heavy cloathing is not wanted, and light clothes may be had cheap of seamen homeward-bound, who want a little grog when they come on shore. All sorts of money go here except coures, which go no where but at Bengal. The reader will see by the following table that the sun's declination is increased 16 degrees between the 22d. of September (when he is on the equator) and the 6th of November (when he is vertical here) which is only 46 days, both included; and in the remaining 45½ days till he arrive on the tropic, he has only 7 deg. 29 min. difference of declination to make; which proves the earth's orbit to be an ellipsis as before observed, otherwise there must be a variation in her speed.

Ascension is a small uninhabited island, which lies N. W. northerly from St Helena, distant about 228 leagues; (for here a mile of longitude is as 58½ to 60) It was probably first discovered on Ascension day, from whence it derived its name; and although it is a steril spot and produces hardly any thing of vegetation, it has its use, and is often touched at by ships navigating those seas for catching tortoise and other fish, which are here very plentiful. The tortoises are caught thus – A number of men go on shore and listen for them coming in from the sea, which they do in great shoals; and after suffering them to land, they run down so as to avoid their throwing sand and pebbles in their eyes with their fins as they pursue them; and keeping from their heads to shun their biting, they put their hands under their shells and turn them on their backs, and leave them to pursue others – see Carthagena. Report informs us of a tortler having fallen asleep and been left behind when his ship was getting under weigh, who subsisted on raw tortoise, drinking their blood when no rain fell, till another ship arrived at the island and took him on board.

The three following tables shew, first, the situation of the places I sailed to or frequented, in rotation, as I came to them; where observe the letters N. S. E. and W. denote north or south latitude and east or west longitude, as they are differently annexed. Secondly, the time when the sun is on any of their several meridians, either before or after he is on the meridian of London: The letters A. M. denoting afore mid-day at London, and P. M. past mid-day or afternoon there. And thirdly, on what days he is vertical or immediately over-head in the several places mentioned, which are situated within the torrid zone, which happens twice a year.

TABLE I.

	deg.	min.	deg.	min.
Narva,	59	08 N.	29	18 E.
Elsinore,	56	00	13	23
Ripperwick,	59	25	10	30
Gottenburg,	57	42	11	44

	deg.	min.	deg.	min.
Coquet Island,	55	22	01	21 W.
Havre-de-Grace,	49	30	00	17 E.
Madeira,	32	25	17	21 W.
Barbadoes,	13	00	59	50
Antigua,	16	57	61	56
Montserrat,	16	37	62	13
Rodonda,	16	55	62	20
Nevis,	17	03	62	42
St Kit's,	17	15	62	50
New York,	41	05	74	51
Port Royal,	17	40	76	37
Jamaica, middle of,	18	08	77	31
Carthagena,	10	27	75	21
Porto Bello,	09	33	79	45
Granadilles,	18	25	89	13
Cape Florida,	25	50	80	20
Charles-Town,	33	22	79	50
Dublin,	53	12	06	55
Cork,	51	45	07	30
Douglas,	54	07	04	42
Belleisle,	47	21	03	13
Port L'Orient,	47	45	03	18
Quiberon,	47	34	03	05
Louisbourg,	45	54	59	50
Quebec,	46	55	69	48
Cape Race,	46	50	50	50
Hamburg,	53	41	10	38 E.
Cape Pinas,	43	51	c6	14 W.
Crocatoa Island,	06	08 S.	105	15 E.
Batavia,	06	12	106	43
Edam,	06	08	106	57
Prince's Island,	06	24	104	48
Madrass,	13	08 N.	80	39
Cape of Good Hope,	34	30 S.	18	37
Cape-Town,	33	55	18	39
St Helena,	16	00	05	53 W.
Ascension,	07	57	13	54

Table II.

	ho.	min.	sec.
Narva,	1	57	12 A. M.
Elsinore,	0	53	32
Ripperwick,	0	42	00
Gottenburg,	0	46	56
Coquet Island,	0	5	24 P. M.
Havre-de-Grace,	0	1	8 A. M.
Madeira,	1	9	24 P. M.
Barbadoes,	3	59	20
Antigua,	4	7	44
Montserrat,	4	8	52
Rodonda,	4	9	20
Nevis,	4	10	48
St Kit's,	4	11	20
New York,	4	59	24
Port Royal,	5	6	28
Jamaica, middle of,	5	12	12
Carthagena,	5	1	24
Porto Bello,	5	19	0
Granadilles,	5	56	52
Cape Florida,	5	21	20
Charles-Town,	5	19	20
Dublin,	0	26	40
Cork,	0	30	0
Douglas,	0	18	48
Belleisle,	0	12	52
Port L'Orient,	0	13	12
Quiberon,	0	12	20
Louisbourg,	3	59	20
Quebec,	4	39	12
Cape Race,	3	23	20
Hamburg,	0	42	32 A. M.
Cape Pinas,	0	24	56 P. M.
Crocatoa Island,	7	0	28 A. M.
Batavia,	7	6	52

	ho.	min.	sec.
Edam,	7	7	48
Prince's Island,	6	59	12
Madrass,	5	22	36
Cape of Good Hope,	1	14	20
Cape-Town,	1	14	28
St Helena,	0	23	32 P. M.
Ascension,	0	55	36

ho.	min.	sec.	
7	7	48 A. M.	
5	56	52 P. M.	
13	4	40	of time, answering to 196 degrees, 10 minutes, which is 16 deg. 10 min. or 970 miles above a semicircle or half round the globe.

TABLE III.

Barbadoes,	Apr. 24	and Aug. 18
Antigua,	May 8	– Aug. 4
Montserrat,	May 7	– Aug. 5
Rodonda,	May 8	– Aug. 4
Nevis,	May 8	– Aug. 4
St Kit's,	May 9	– Aug. 3
Port Royal,	May 10	– Aug. 2
Jamaica, middle of,	May 11	– Aug. 1
Granadilles,	May 13	– July 30
Crocatoa Island,	Oct. 8	– Mar. 5
Batavia,	Oct. 9	– Mar. 4
Edam,	Oct. 9	– Mar. 4
Prince's Island,	Oct. 9	– Mar. 4
Madrass,	Apr. 25	– Aug. 17
St Helena,	Nov. 6	– Feb. 5
Ascension,	Oct. 13	– Mar. 1

An Explanation of Nautical Terms

I now come to explain some of the nautical terms or names and expressions made use of in the sea-service, which are not familiar to persons unacquainted with the sea; and as to the geographical ones, I have been so plain in treating of the science itself that there needs no further explanation, although it was mentioned in my proposals.

Afore, Forward or before.

Abaft, Toward the stern or after-part of the ship.

Amain, Let run or let go suddenly all at once.

Aloft, In the top or at the mast head, &c.

Anchor, The instrument by which the ship rides.

Avaft, Stop, stay, or leave off.

Athwart, Across or cross-way.

Bale, To throw water out, or a package of goods.

Back-stays, Part of the standing-rigging to keep the mast aft.

Ballast, Weight to bring a ship down in the water.

Barge, A boat with ten or twelve oars.

Bearing, The way a ship or place bears of you.

Bearings of a ship, The swell of her bows, bulges, and counters, whereby she bears her burden.

Bearing up, or rather *Bearing away*, Going more from the wind or veering to leeward.

Beam, or *Abeam*, Opposed to the side or beam ends.

Belay, To make fast or secure a rope or fall, &c.

Bend, To apply to and fasten a sail or other thing.

Birth, A place for a ship or a station for a man, &c.

Bight of a rope, The middle, when the ends are fast.

Bight, A narrow corner of a bay or river.

Bilge, To stave or break a plank under the bulge.

Binnacle, A place for the compasses to stand in.

Bits, Pieces of timber to fasten the cable to, &c.

Bonnet, Additional piece of canvass fixed to a sail.

Board, To run along side a vessel and jump in sword in hand to force a surrender.

Break bulk, To open the hold and take goods out.

Battens, Thin pieces of wood which are placed on either side the fish of a lower mast; also laths to nail round the combings to secure the tarpaulings

Bouy, A floating mark fixed on a rock or shoal.

Blocks, Pieces of wood of various sizes, with one, two, or more sheaves in them to reeve ropes thro' for making purchases, working the sails, &c.

Braces, Ropes fixed at the yard-arms wherewith they are swung and pointed forward and aft.

Bomkins, Two pieces of timber projecting from the sides of the stem for the fore-tasks to haul down to

Bowsprit, A large piece of timber which stands peaking forward over the stem.

Bulk head, A partition or barricado.

Bolt-rope, A rope or pieces of rope which go round a sail to prevent it splitting and being of different sizes; the parts are distinguished by head-rope, foot-rope, and leach-ropes.

Bow-lines, Ropes fastened with bridles to cringles in the leach-ropes of the sails to haul them forward.

Bunt-lines, For the purpose of hauling up the foot of courses, top-sails, or topgallant-sails.

Broach to, To bring the ship suddenly up into the wind when she was going large, and thereby laying her athwart the trough of the sea.

Bridle, A cable fastened to a chain for harbour moorings.

Chase, A pursuit. *To chase*, To pursue. *The chase*, The vessel pursued.

Careening, Giving a ship a heel or inclination to one side.

Caulking, Filling the seams with oakum.

Cun, or *Con*, To direct the helm's man in steering.

Course, Point of the compass on which the ship sails.

Courses, The lower sails, viz. sprit-sail, fore-sail, main-sail, mizzen, and spanker.

Cockswain, A person who steers a barge, &c.

Chains, Places projecting from the ship's sides for the lower shrouds to fasten to by chains or plates secured to the sides with bolts.

Chestrees, Timbers to haul the main-tacks down to.

Chain-pumps, Machines wrought by winches, which will throw up a tun of water in a minute. Every large ship has four of these, and others two.

Cap, A piece of wood which goes over a mast head for the top-mast to go through.

Capstan, An instrument that is turned round with bars to purchase anchors with &c.

Cable's-length, A hundred and twenty fathoms.

Catharpins, A purchase to contine the lower shrouds together so as to allow for bracing up the yards.

Cat-heads, Two timbers which project sideways from the bows to purchase the anchors from the hawse, &c.

Capsize, To turn upside down or end for end.

Clews, Bights of the bolt-rope served at the lower corners of the sails to which the tacks, sheats, &c. are fastened for working or furling them.

Clew-garnets, Purchases for hauling up the clews of the courses.

Clew-lines, Ditto for the top and topgallant sails.

Cross-jack, A sail set on the mizzen-mast with a square yard.

Crank, Top heavy or apt to heel to the wind.

Cutter, A boat with six oars.

Dead water, The eddy under the ship's stern.

Douce, To strike or haul down suddenly.

Dead lights, Shutters for the cabin windows.

Dead wind, Wind blowing from the point towards which the ship wants to go; wind in our teeth.

Dead-eyes, Blocks with holes to reeve the lanyards of the shrouds and back-stays through.

Drift, The way the ship drives and the rate she drives at when laying to, or when her anchor comes home.

Driver, A sail set at the mizzen peak when the ship is going large.

Ensign-staff, A staff to hoist the ensign on, hanging over the stern in a line with the stern-post.

End-for-end, A term used when a rope is unreeved.

Fathom, A measure of six feet.

Fake, A circle of a rope or cable quoiled.

Furl, To roll up and bind the sails to the yards.

Fish, A piece of wood that goes up the fore part of the lower masts; also pieces applied to strengthen a mast that is sprung.

Fish for the anchor, Includes the davit, a piece of timber which rigs out from the fore-castle, with the collar, pendant, book, and tackle, for getting the flukes of the anchor up.

Fid, A square piece of wood or iron which goes through the heel of a top-mast of topgallant-mast and rests with its ends on the trullel-trees to support it.

Fore castle, A short deck reaching a little abast the fore-mast.

Flag-staves, Spaces at the mast head to hoist flags.

Gage, The ship's draught of water, or the depth she draws.

Great cabin, An appartment for the Captain.

Ground tackle, Anchors, grapnels, cables, &c.

Gammon the bowsprit, Securing it by many turns of a piece of strong cordage passed over it and through a ring-bolt in the stem.

Gun-room, A division of the lower deck abaft.

Gunnel, or *Gunwale*, The timbers that encompass the ship's sides fore and aft.

Gaskets, Platted pieces made of old ropes to furl the sails to the yards with.

Helm, The machine by which the ship is steered, including the rudder, tiller, wheel, and wheel rope, in one general term.

Helm's-a-lee, That is, the tiller is quite down.

Hard-a-weather, To put the helm quite to windward

Haul, Pull down.

Heave at the capstan, Heave round by thrusting at the bars; heave and paul.

Heave down, To heave the ship on her broad-side.

Heave of the sea, The power the swell has on a ship to drive her out of, or faster on in her course; it is sometimes called the send of the sea.

Hail, To call to the crew on board another ship.

Halyards, Ropes by which the sails or colours are hoisted.

Hatchways, Places for goods, &c. to go down.

Hause-holes, Two holes on each side the stem for the cables to pass through, which are plugged up at sea when the cables are unbent.

Hawser, A small cable to use with a kedge-anchor.

Heel, Inclining to one side; the after-part of the keel is also called the heel, and the fore end the fore foot.

Hitch, To take a turn or fasten a rope.

Hoist, To haul, sway, or run up a sail, colours, &c.

Horses, Ropes leading from the yard-arms inward to walk out on.

Hold, The space between the orloop-deck and the floor of the bottom; It is distinguished in parts as fore-hold, main-hold, and after-hold, and in these the stores are stowed (and cargo if a merchant ship) and in the fore part and on the orloop is the magazine, with the Boatswain, Gunner, and Carpenter's store-rooms and sail-room; and in the after-part, the lazaretta, cock-pit, steward's room, and bread-room.

Hull, The body of a ship; and when the masts are out, it is called a hulk.

Jeers, Ropes for swaying up and suspending the lower yards.

Jibb, A sail set on a boom rigged out from the bowsprit end.

Jolly-boat, A small boat with two oars.

Keel, A timber extended fore and aft along the bottom of a vessel and projecting below it.

Large, Going from the wind.

Larboard, The left side when you face forward.

Labours, The ship rolls or pitches sharp and sudden.

Land-fall, Making or discovering land.

Land-locked, Sheltered with land nearly all round, or entangled with land that cannot be cleared.

Lanyards, Ropes to set up and secure the shrouds.

Leeward, The way the wind blows.

Lee-gage, Fighting an enemy that is to windward.

Lee shore, A shore toward which the wind blows.

Leack-lines, Lines to haul up the leaches of the courses.

Lifts, Ropes to support and elevate or lower the yard-arms.

Live, Keep from sinking in a great sea-gale.

Luff, or *Loofe*, To bring the ship nearer the wind.

Long-boat, A large boat or launch to bring off stores, water, &c.

Lurching, Laying down to the wind suddenly.

Masts, Timbers that support the yards and sails.

Mizzen, A sail that hauls out aft from the mizzen mast.

Moor, To secure the ship with two anchors, lying one each way.

Make a board, To put about and come on the other tack or with the other side to the wind.

No-man's-land, A space between the heels of the booms.

Nun-bouy, A kind of cask fastened to the crown of an anchor to give notice where it lies, with a bouy-rope strong enough to weigh the anchor occasionally.

Neaps, The tides at the first and last quarters of the moon.

Oakum, Old ropes unraveled to caulk with.

Offing, Off from the land or distance.

Over-haul, To disentangle or clear away; also to come up with a vessel we are pursuing.

Pey, To run pitch in the seams; also to besmear the bottom, sides, or lower masts, with pitch, tallow and brimstone, tar and ochre, varnish, &c.

Pinnace, A curval-built boat with eight oars.

Pomillion, A pommel on the breech of a gun for the breeching-thimble to seize to.

Points, Platted ropes for reefing the sails.

Ports, Holes for the guns to run out at, &c.

Port, A word used for the larboard-side; also a haven, &c.

Purchase, To weigh an anchor, sway up or hoist.

Quoil, To lay up a rope in a round form clear for running.

Quarter, A part of the ship between the mizzen chains and the stern-post.

Quarters, The stations of the people at the guns, small-arms, &c. in time of action.

Rake, To fire fore and aft; also the inclination of the stern and masts.

Reeve, To put a rope through a block or dead-eye,

Reef, To take up part of a sail in order to make it less when there is too much wind.

Reef, A range of rocks, or a sand-bank; the latter is called a bar where it lays across a river.

Reach, Part of a river between two points of land that lie in a right line with each other.

Ride at anchor, The anchors keeping a ship from driving out of her station.

Road, A place for a ship to lie at anchor.

Rat-lines, Lines going across the shrouds for steps to go aloft by.

Shrouds, Ropes by which the masts are secured sideways.

Strike, To yield to an enemy.

Stiff, Not crank or apt to yield to the wind.

Settle, To lower or ease off halyards, &c.

Sheer, Shape; also a direction given by the helm when riding at anchor.

Scud, To run right before the wind when there is too much for the ship's keeping her course.

Spill, To shiver the sails in the wind.

Spring tides, Those at the full and change of the moon.

Sound, A deep bay; also to get ground with the lead.

Starboard, The right-hand side.

Steady, A word used to direct the helm's man in steering a ship before the wind.

Standing, Running or going in any direction, &c.

Stays, Strong ropes leading forward to secure the masts from going aft.

State-room, An apartment abast under the poop.

Stem, A strong bowed timber extending from the keel up between the bows and connecting the bow-timbers, and to which the cut-water and head are secured.

Stem, To stop against the tide or current.

Shank-painter, A rope and chain to secure the flukes of an anchor.

Stoppers, Ropes to make fast the stock part of an anchor; others to stopper cables, &c.

Tack, To put about head to wind.

Tacks, Strong ropes to confine the foot of a sail forward while it is expanded aft by the contrary sheat.

Tarpauling, A tarred cloth to nail over the hatchway.

Taunt, Lofty or high rigged.

Tow, To draw or drag a ship with a tow-line after another that is stronger and can out-sail her.

Trunnions, Projections on which the gun rests in a carriage.

Tompions, Plugs for the muzzles of the guns.

Tier, A row of guns fore and aft, or of casks in the hold.

Top, A sort of plat-form which goes over the lower mast heads to give an angle to the top-mast shrouds.

Trussel-trees, Two pieces of timber placed on the cheeks of a lower mast to support the cross-trees, top, and the weight of the top-mast, &c.

Under way, Loose from her anchors with some sail set.

Veer away, To surge or let out cable, hawser, &c.

Veers, The wind veers round or shifts; veers and hauls.

Wake, The track the ship describes in the water.

Wales, Timbers that go round the ship at her water-course; and the mark the water makes on them is called the water-line or lines.

Weather, To go to windward of a ship or land. &c.

Weather-gage, To engage an enemy under our lee.

Windlas, A roller to purchase anchors with.

Were, or *Veer ship*, To veer her round before the wind and bring her on the other tack.

Ward-room, An apartment for the Lieutenants.

Warp, To heave a vessel in with a kedge and towline.

Weigh, To get up an anchor. &c.

Yawl, A boat with six oars.

Yaws, Goes in and out, does not steer steady.

Yards, Spars on which the sails are spread out.

The Seaman's Narrative Resumed

I must now for a moment resume my narrative. After being discharged at Chatham, I repaired to London to enquire after my prize-money, and found that some of it had been paid into the treasury of Greenwich hospital through the neglect of my attorney, who had not applied for it in due time; and the remainder being got into the hands of Mr William Daniel, by virtue of a power made to him some time before, he deceived me by producing a false paper, which gave me a prospect of receiving my money in about 6 months. So as though nature had placed a kind of sympathy between us and the place of our nativity, I left London and came down into Lincolnshire. 'Now all the storms and dangers o'er, cast anchor on my native shore,' but so much disabled, that I knew not how to earn a shilling. Shortly after, I received a letter from my messmate, William Newton, advising me to look after Mr Daniel, as he apprehended him likely to get into Fleet prison for debt; on which I applied to Mr G. J—d, attorney at law in this town, desiring him, on the caution given in Newton's letter, to write about it immediately, which he promised; but neglecting to do it for about 8 weeks, it was then too late, for Mr Daniel had got into the Fleet, and 4 years after received the benefit of an insolvent act, by which I lost 281. It now became necessary to consider how I should obtain a livelihood in future: I had some thought of teaching school; but being diffident of my abilities for such an undertaking, because I could not write well, I engaged myself to Mr F. Singleton of Louth to learn the art of making gloves and leather breeches: At the expiration of the time agreed for, I married a wife, and with her removed to Horncastle; and having to appear at Chatham in 1769, I left my wife at Horncastle and went and worked at Bow with Mr S. Fields, where I became a genuine type of a journey-man breeches-maker: for my shoes being worn out with the journey up to London, I could not keep them on without kicking them against the posts as I passed along the streets, till at length I got 2s. 6d. of my Mrs and bought a second-hand pair in rag fair. After I had passed the review at the Chest in April 1769, I returned to

Horncastle and worked for Mr John Oldham; and in October 1770, removed to Louth with my wife and daughter, and served the late Mr R. Chapman and his several successors, till July 1789; since which, I have served every person who pleased to favour me with his commands, and with ever to merit the continuance of their esteem and acknowledge their favours. I had again to appear at Chatbam in April 1774: In April 1778, when my pension was reduced to 5l. In June 1780: In May 1785: And in April 1788; when on my return by the Lincoln coach, I was very much hurt by its being overturned near the Green Man inn on Finchley common on the evening of the 2nd, of April, and might have perished on the road, as Mrs. T–rl–ne refused to take me in, but for the humanity of a gentleman inside passenger, who insisted on my being taken in and attended to; on which Mr Taylor of Whetstone was sent for, who bled me and applied something to the bruise; and next day I was sent to St. Bartholomew's hospital, where being placed under the care of surgeons Pitt and London, I got better in 29 days; and by means of the aforesaid gentleman, I also received some recompense of Mr Boulton at the Golden-cross Charing-cross for my loss of time, and arrived at Louth May the 10th. I appeared in April 1791, and shortly after my leg seemed to be worse; for part of the fibula, which was carious, having been extracted by Dr Young at Madras in 1764, the substance brought over the remaining part of it was a spongy kind of flesh, and sometimes would break out, which now became rather ulcerous again; nevertheless I kept it under until the latter end of 1792, when it began to emit a small discharge of black matter so as to stain the plaister a little; on which I applied to a gentleman who attended me gratis for 9 weeks; and on the 28th of January 1793, descerning the bone to be divided, I said to him, Dr my leg's in two, what must I do? He said, you must get some other advice! Horror seized my mind, being brought to the single alternative of either a lingering and excruciating pain which must terminate in death, or suffer the amputation of my limb: So I sent for Mr T. Wilson, surgeon, Warden of this corporation, (now Dr Wilson of Grantham) who came and inspected the sore, and generously used every means in his power to effect a cure and save the leg, had it been possible; and calling in the advice of other professional gentlemen, Messrs. Wrigglesworth, Petener, and King, he at first (on the 14th of February) performed an operation on the ankle by cutting off the flesh that he might extract the carious bone; which means proving ineffectual, he, assisted by Mr Petener and Mr King, with their several assistants, performed the amputation on the 24th of May, 1793, in the 58th year of my life and the 30th of my lameness. All this, with the attendance given till a cure was made of my stump, Mr Wilson generously performed gratis. To the humanity of these gentlemen, together with the humane and benevolent ladies, gentlemen, and other charitable inhabitants of this town and vicinity, (under the providential hand of God, whose goodness extends to the utmost bounds of his creation) I owe my preservation and present existence, as they so liberally administered to my relief and the support of my family under the pressure of my affliction and misfortune; for which undeserved, unexpected, and exceeding great favours, may God's everlasting love through the merits of his Son Jesus rest upon every individual of them; and while I live I shall ever esteem them as my kind benefactors and preservers, and myself their very humble and thankful servant.

William Spavens.

DECEMBER 5, 1793.

I appeared to review at Chatham again on the 1st of April 1794, when the governors of the Chest thought good to augment my pension to six pounds and a mark (the limb being off below the knee) commencing from Midsummer 1793, and gave me a ticket for five years, agreeable to the rules of the Chest.

The Invalid, *an Anecdote*

Being come out of Hazlar hospital in November 1765, lame and swinging on a pair of crutches, in a dress that likewise bespoke me an invalided seaman, or one of those whom fate had bloomed to beg bitter bread 'through realms their valour sav'd,' as I knocked at a door in Cold Harbour, Gosport, a servant girl came and said, 'we give nothing away here;' I said, you was asked for nothing; but pray can you tell me where Elizabeth Newton lives? She disdainfully said no, unless she lives in Cross-street. This made me reflect how different a man I now seemed to be from what I had been: I thought how much. I now differed from that gay and sprightly youth who used to trip along the streets of Gosport, at the sight of whom the blushing fair would innocently gaze and smile as he

passed by, and envy almost kindle in the breast of her who saw me
with another lass in tow! I now might truly say, 'if thou art he, but
ah! how fall'n.' The contrast seemed as great as that between the
bright-sided *Neptune* with all ataunt and her colours streaming in
the wind, and the old *Blenheim*-hospital ship with pieces of plaister
and poultice-clothes sticking to her wales, having nothing standing
except her ensign-staff. Such are the vicissitudes of human life,
particularly among the sons of Neptune and Mars!!!

Index

Page numbers in italics refer to tables.
Abbreviations: Cdre = Commodore; Fr = French; GB = British merchant ship; HMS = His Majesty's Ship; Lt = Lieutenant; Neth = Netherlands; R/A = Rear-Admiral; V/A = Vice-Admiral.

Also in the *Sailors' Tales* Series:
Nelsonian Reminiscences
by Lt G. S. Parsons

George Samuel Parsons entered the Royal Navy in 1795 and although he never rose above the rank of Lieutenant, before he was invalided out of the service in 1810 he had seen a remarkable amount of action. He was present at the great fleet battle of St Vincent in 1797, was involved in the successful invasion of Egypt in 1801, and commanded a number of daring cutting-out expeditions later. However, he was proudest of his time in the *Foudroyant* in 1798, when he served under Nelson himself. Naturally, the historical interest centres on this association, especially as it covers the hero's much-criticised years at the corrupt court of Naples.

Luckily for posterity, Parsons was an acute and independent observer, and his views are often surprising and full of insight. He could also tell a good story, and there is no shortage of humorous observations, like Sir Sidney Smith's diet of rats.

For anyone whose interest in the period has been whetted by the fiction of Patrick O'Brian or C S Forester, this is the real-life equivalent.

216 x 138mm, 200pp, £9.95 paperback
ISBN 186176 084 1

For an illustrated catalogue of all Chatham Publishing books, contact:
The Marketing Department, Chatham Publishing
61 Frith Street, London W1V 5TA
Tel: 0171 434 4242 Fax: 0171 434 4415